The Story of Zhang Jian

漫话张謇

外文出版社
FOREIGN LANGUAGES PRESS

First Edition 2021

ISBN 978-7-119-12812-2

Published by Foreign Languages Press Co. Ltd

24 Baiwanzhuang Road, Beijing 100037, China

Distributed by China International Book Trading Corporation

35 Chegongzhuang Xilu, Beijing 100044, China

P.O. Box 399, Beijing, China

Printed in the People's Republic of China

民 族 企 业 家 的 楷 模

A Paragon of Patriotism, A Model of Entrepreneurship

前言

雄伟壮丽的长江，从远古的雪山走来，跳跃奔涌6300公里后注入大海。而在长江最终追寻到大海的地方，坐落着南通这座古老而又年轻的城市。江海奔流、沃野千里，敢于追梦、善于圆梦的江海儿女在这里创造了一个又一个神奇。在这些伟大的创造中，一个伟大的人物出现了。纵使时光逝去百年，他的名字仍在江海大地上镌刻，他的创造至今仍触摸可及，他的精神仍被在新时代称颂，他就是张謇。

百余年前，清末状元张謇怀揣实业救国的梦想，在家乡南通兴实业、办教育、发展各类社会事业，一座江海之城开启了近现代文明的征程，缔造了堪称“中国近代第一城”的辉煌。中华人民共和国成立后,毛泽东主席曾说：“讲轻工业，不能忘记张謇。”习近平总书记称赞张謇说：“提倡实干兴邦，起而行之，兴办了一系列实业、教育、医疗、社会公益事业，帮助群众，造福乡梓，是我国民族企业家的楷模。”“要把南通博物苑和张謇故居作为爱国主义教育基地，让广大民营企业家和青少年受到教育，增强社会责任感，坚定‘四个自信’。”

为了让海内外更多人知晓张謇、了解张謇，真切感受中华文化熏陶出来的知识分子的社会担当和人文情怀，我们选取了张謇一生中部分重要节点和精彩片段，以漫画的形式加以呈现，编成此书。囿于时间和水平关系，书中不当之处敬希读者指正。

编者

2021年7月

Preface

The majestic Yangtze River, originated from Snow Mountain, rages forward for 6300 km before flowing into the sea. At the end of its journey sits an ancient yet modern city, Nantong. For thousands of years, the city has witnessed numerous record-breaking moments, among which the life journey of a great man is especially noteworthy. Even a hundred years later, his name is still engraved on our mind, his creation is still around us, and his spirit is still applauded by people in the new era. The great man is Zhang Jian.

More than a hundred years ago, Zhang Jian, the top-notch scholar in the late Qing Dynasty, strove to realize his dream of saving the country by developing industry. He committed himself to developing industries while boosting education and various social undertakings in his hometown Nantong. Under his leadership, Nantong, later known as the pioneering city in modern China, twisted through its way to modernity. After the founding of new China, Chairman Mao Zedong once commented, "When talking about light industry, we can't forget Zhang Jian." General Secretary of the CPC Central Committee Xi Jinping commended Zhang Jian for his advocacy of "doing solid work to revive the nation", and praised him for establishing a series of industrial, educational, medical, and social undertakings for the well-being of the people and the community, regarding him as a paragon of patriotism and a model of entrepreneurship. General Secretary Xi also gave instructions that Nantong Museum and Zhang Jian's former residence should be used as bases to promote patriotism and educate the vast number of private entrepreneurs and young people to enhance their sense of social responsibility, and strengthen their confidence in the path, theory, system, and culture of socialism with Chinese characteristics.

To let more people at home and abroad know about Zhang Jian, and appreciate the social responsibility and humanistic care shown by intellectuals under the influence of Chinese culture, we have selected some important episodes and highlights of Zhang Jian's life, and presented them in the form of comic book. Comments from the readers are highly appreciated.

Editor

July 2021

目录 Contents

我踏金鳌海上来

I Came from the Sea, Riding on the Golden Turtle

敢为天下先

A Bold Pioneer

国家兴亡，匹夫有责

Everyone Has a Stake in the Rise and Fall of the Nation

强毅之力，利民之智

Fighting with an Indomitable Will to Enlighten the People

竞会五洲文明

Competing and Cooperating with the Outside World

张謇

张謇（1853—1926）字季直，号啬庵，江苏南通人，晚清状元，近代伟大的爱国者，著名实业家、教育家、社会活动家。

张謇是中国近代“实业救国”思想的代表人物，是民族棉纺织工业的奠基人之一。他创办的以大生纺织公司为核心的企业集团是近代民族工业的翘楚；他开发滩涂，改良盐业，推广植棉和棉种改良，推动了苏北沿海棉垦区的形成；他倡导“教育救国”，在南通构建了较完整的基础教育体系，创办了一批职业学校和高等学校；他积极倡导支持科学普及和技术应用；他担任民国政府农商总长期间，主持颁布实施了一系列政策、法令以促进国民经济发展；他以“地方自治”为号召，对南通进行了全方位的经营，使南通从一个落后小邑转变成一个名闻遐迩的近代工商业城市。张謇的爱国主张和救国实践对中国近代化进程产生了持久深远的影响，被誉为爱国企业家的典范、民族企业家的楷模。

The Story of Zhang Jian

Zhang Jian (1853–1926), a native of Nantong, Jiangsu Province, is a patriotic industrialist, educator and social activist of great renown in modern times.

As a proponent of "saving the country by developing industry" in modern China, he participated in founding national cotton textile industry. His business conglomerate, revolving around Dasheng Textile Company, was the national industry leader. He enabled the formation of the cotton reclamation area in northern Jiangsu coast by developing mudflats, reshaping the salt industry, improving cotton seed and promoting cotton planting. Championing the idea of "education for national salvation", he set up integrated system for basic education and founded a number of vocational schools and schools for higher education. He actively supported the popularization of science and application of technology. During his tenure as minister of agriculture and commerce in the government of the Republic of China, he presided over the promulgation and implementation of a series of policies and decrees to revive national economy. Upholding the idea of "self-governance at local level", he expertly managed Nantong, transforming it from a small backward county into a well-known modern industrial and commercial city. Zhang Jian's patriotic ideas and the practice of national salvation had a lasting and far-reaching impact on the modernization of China. He is regarded as a paragon of patriotism and a model of entrepreneurship.

我 踏 金 鳌 海 上 来

I Came from the Sea,
Riding on the Golden Turtle

年少显峥嵘

1853年，张謇出生于海门常乐镇一个农商兼作的小户人家，排行第四。其父张彭年十分重视儿子们的教育，送他们在邻近私塾读书。4岁时张謇背诵《千字文》，竟然一字无误，10岁时已经读完了《大学》《中庸》《论语》《孟子》等儒家经典著作。

11岁时，张父聘请西亭老秀才宋蓬山在家里给几个儿子授课，主要学习五言诗、试帖诗。13岁时，张謇居然能够“制艺成篇”了。一天，张父与宋蓬山正在闲谈，见一人骑白马从大门外走过，宋老先生随口出个七字对“人骑白马门前去”，张謇未加思索，即以“我踏金鳌海上来”对之。对仗工整，张父和老师大喜。此对也被传为张謇未来高中状元的征兆。

Showing Promise at a Young Age

In 1853, Zhang Jian was born to a humble family in the town of Changle in Haimen. He was the fourth child. His father, Zhang Pengnian, attached great importance to the education of his sons. When Zhang Jian was four years old, he recited the *Thousand-Character Classic* (Children's primer in ancient China) without making a single mistake, so his father sent him to study with his brothers in a neighboring old-style private school.

When Zhang Jian reached eleven, his father hired Song Pengshan, an elderly scholar from Xiting town, to give lessons to his sons at home. By the age of thirteen, Zhang Jian was able to write stereotyped essays required for imperial examination. One day, when Zhang's father and Song Pengshan were having a casual conversation, they saw a man on a white horse passing by the gate. At the sight of the scene, Mr. Song made a seven-character pair of “A man passed by the gate, riding on the white horse”. Zhang Jian, without hesitation, replied “I came from the sea, riding on the golden turtle” (golden turtle is an auspicious supernatural being). Zhang's father and teacher were very pleased with the neatness of the couplet. This pair is also said to be an omen that Zhang Jian would be the top scorer in the imperial civil examination.

九百九十九

同治五年（1866），宋蓬山去世。张謇与三哥张詧来到通州西亭宋氏私塾，开始了在西亭5年的求学生涯。在宋家读书期间，张謇发愤刻苦，每夜读书“必尽油二盏”，一心想通过科举来获得“功名”。

次年，15岁的张謇开始走上科考之路。初上考场，张謇在县试、州试中均顺利通过。但是州试成绩欠佳，名次在第二百余名。其师宋璞斋训斥他说：“假使有一千人去考试，要取九百九十九人，只有一个不取，就是你！”张謇听后，非常难过，在住处写下 “九百九十九”五个大字。从此发愤自励，苦熬六个月之后，同年10月的院试，张謇被取中第26名附学生员，获得秀才名号。

Nine Hundred and Ninety Nine

In 1866 (the sixth year under the reign of Tongzhi Emperor in Qing Dynasty), Song Pengshan passed away. Zhang Jian and his third brother Zhang Cha went to the private school of Song's family in Xiting town. During his stay in that school, Zhang Jian was so hardworking that he would "exhaust the oil of two lamps" every night for studying, and he was determined to obtain "merit" through the imperial examination.

In 1867, at the age of 15, Zhang Jian started his journey to the imperial examinations. He passed the first two exams of the three entry-level exams in the imperial examination, but his ranking was not outstanding, at about 200th some place. His teacher, Song Puzhai, reprimanded him, saying, "If there are a thousand people taking the exam, of whom nine hundred and ninety nine will be taken, you will be the only one that won't be taken!" Hearing this, Zhang Jian was dismayed and wrote down five big words "九百九十九" (the Chinese characters of nine hundred and ninety nine) in his residence. After six months of hard work, Zhang Jian won the 26th place in the last examination the three entry-level exams, being awarded the title of "Xiu Cai".

冒籍之灾

按照科举旧俗，祖上三代没有学官或入学为生员者，被称为“冷籍”，其子弟很难报考，并易遭受歧视。张謇即为“冷籍”。为让张謇顺利参加科考，张彭年便采纳老师的建议，冒充如皋人张驹之孙，改名为“育才”在如皋应试。此后，张謇通过了县试、州试、院试，获得秀才称号。

然而，冒籍考试却带来了一系列的麻烦，张驹家人借此向张彭年大加勒索，此后5年，张家负债达千两之多，一个小康之家几乎倾家荡产。张謇饱受摧残，经历了其人生的第一次磨难。

后在海门训导赵菊泉、通州知州孙云锦这些正直官员帮助下，经礼部核准，张謇学籍于1873年被划归通州，才结束了这场无妄之灾。

The Imposture Affair

According to the usual practice of the imperial examinations, it was difficult for those whose ancestors had not studied for three generations to sit imperial examination. As Zhang Jian was in such a condition, his father took the advice of his teacher that Zhang Jian pretended to be the grandson of Zhang Ju, a native of Rugao, and changed his name to “Yucai” to take the examination in Rugao. After that, Zhang Jian passed the three entry-level exams in the imperial examination and was awarded the title “Xiu Cai”.

However, the deception brought about rippling troubles as Zhang Ju’s family used it to blackmail Zhang Pengnian. In the ensuing five years, a large sum of fortune was extorted from Zhang Jian’s family, which left the comfortably-off family in debt. Zhang Jian himself was also traumatized by the experience.

Fortunately, Haimen instructor Zhao Juquan and Tongzhou Magistrate Sun Yunjin offered to get Zhang Jian out of the predicament. And finally in 1873, Zhang Jian was reregistered as Tongzhou scholar with the approval of the Ministry of Rites. It was till then that the imposture affair was mitigated.

初露头角

1875年，张謇结识了庆军统领吴长庆。次年，张謇入吴长庆幕府，处理日常文字工作。1880年，张謇随吴长庆移驻山东登州，写下“微闻玉帛方修好，却倚危阑日听涛”的诗句，表达了他对当前海防部署的担忧。1882年，朝鲜发生“壬午兵变”，张謇随吴长庆入朝达两年之久。在此期间，张謇常常夜以继日地“理画前敌军事”，参与庆军历次重大决策，协助吴长庆迅速有效地解决了朝鲜的内乱，并挫败了日本吞并朝鲜的企图。张謇积极建言献策，撰写了多篇策论文章，对日渐严重的民族危机表现出深重的忧虑。吴长庆对张謇的表现赞赏有加，称“其功自在野战攻城之上……处置如此大事，举重若轻，何等识力器量”！

Revealing Outstanding Talent

In 1875, Zhang Jian befriended Wu Changqing, the commander of the Qing army. The next year, he joined the office of the commander, working on drafting documents. In 1880, Zhang Jian moved to Dengzhou, Shandong Province as the Qing army shifted there for garrison duty. Then he wrote the lines "As I leaned on the rails listening to the sound of roaring sea, I was worried by the ever-deepening national crisis", expressing his concern about the current sea defense deployment. In 1882, a mutiny to topple feudal government erupted in Korea; Zhangjian was sent to Korea by Qing government with Wu Changqing to quell the unrest. During this period, Zhang Jian often spent night and day managing the military affairs of the frontline and participated in deliberating the major decisions of the Qing army, helping Wu Changqing to quickly and effectively solve the civil unrest in Korea and frustrate the Japanese attempt to annex Korea. Zhang Jian was active in offering policy advice and wrote many essays where he expressed deep concern about the growing national crisis. Wu Changqing praised Zhang Jian's performance, saying, "His merits are not limited to military affairs and he handled such an important matter with ease, what knowledge and ability!"

蚕桑摘要

经营乡里

1885年，张謇在京师参加顺天府乡试，高中第二名，称为“南元”。但此后4次参加礼部会试，皆名落孙山，好在张謇并不将科举入仕视为人生的唯一目标，相反产生了“中国振兴实业，其责任须在士大夫”的想法。他在家乡通州，凭借士绅的身份，期望为乡民多办实事。

张謇经营乡里的活动主要有：办理通海花布减捐，推动政府减税，促进通州、海门一带土布业发展；提倡改良和发展蚕桑事业，呼吁两江总督刘坤一“免除丝绢十年，以兴蚕利”，实行就地招商开行收茧，使通海一带形成兴办蚕桑的热潮；还曾办理海门溥善堂、主持瀛洲书院等。

Contributing to His Hometown

In 1885, Zhang Jian passed the triennial provincial-level imperial examination as runner-up. After that, he took metropolitan examinations held by the Ministry of Rites four times, all failed. But Zhang Jian did not consider the imperial examination to be the only goal of his life; instead, he had the idea that “the responsibility of revitalizing industry in China must lie with the scholar.” In his hometown, Tongzhou, he hoped to do more things under his status as a squire (referring to a refined man of good social standing who owns and lives on an estate in rural areas).

Zhang Jian stayed committed to managing his hometown in many aspects. He urged the government to reduce taxes, facilitating the development of the hand-woven cloth industry in Tongzhou and Haimen. He appealed to Liu Kunyi, the governor of Liangjiang (including present Jiangsu, Anhui, and Jiangxi provinces in Qing Dynasty), to exempt tax on silk for ten years to promote sericulture. He also helped to establish cocoon trading companies. In a few years, millions of mulberry trees had been planted in the area of Tonghai, boosting a craze for sericulture. He founded Haimen Benevolent Association and presided over the Yingzhou Academy.

捷報
貴府少大老爺張印謇恭應
殿試一甲第一名
賜進士及第
欽點翰林院修撰
報錄人王上林

高中状元

1894年，为庆祝慈禧太后六十大寿，清廷特设恩科会试。张謇依父命再次踏上赴京师的科考之路。

2月，张謇先于会试中考得第六十名贡士，3月又在礼部复试中得一等第十名，取得殿试资格。4月22日殿试，殿试卷被送入乾清宫西暖阁，请光绪帝过目，翁同龢特地介绍张謇是江南名士，并且是个孝子。光绪闻听大喜，钦定张謇为第一甲第一名，即状元。次日，张謇以被授以翰林院修撰。不久，中日甲午战争爆发，清军节节败退，帝后党争日趋激烈。此间，张謇接到父亲张彭年的去世讯息，便离京回乡。

Top Scorer in the Highest Imperial Examination

In 1894, a special imperial examination was held to celebrate the 60th birthday of the Empress Dowager Cixi. Zhang Jian, following the order of his father, set out to take the examination held in Beijing.

In February that year, Zhang Jian won the 60th place in the metropolitan examination held by the Ministry of Rites, and in March, got the 10th place in the re-examination of the Ministry of Rites, which qualified him for the palace examination (the highest imperial examination). In the palace examination held on April 22, the papers of all the examinees were sent to Emperor Guangxu for review. Weng Tonghe recommended Zhang Jian as a renowned scholar in the South China and stressed his filial piety. Emperor Guangxu was immensely impressed by him and awarded him the title of top scholar through imperial command. On the next day, Zhang Jian was appointed as Editor of Imperial Hanlin Academy. Shortly afterward, the Sino-Japanese War of 1894-1895 broke out. The crushing defeat of the Qing army and the ever-increasing strife between the emperor and the empress dowager made him even more disappointed. Meanwhile, his father Zhang Pengnian passed away. Upon receiving the news, Zhang Jian left Beijing and returned to his hometown.

创立大生

1895年，清政府在内外交困中开始对民间兴办新兴产业大加鼓励。年底，张之洞奏派在籍绅士张謇“总理通海一带商务”，“酌量地方情形，增设纱丝各厂”。张謇经过“反复审虑”，决定“舍身喂虎”，下海经商。从1895年到1899年，经过5年的艰苦创业，一座拥有2万余枚纱锭的近代化纱厂——大生纱厂矗立在长江北岸的唐闸镇。大生纱厂开车之际，翁同龢亲撰对联：“枢机之发，动乎天地；衣被所及，遍我东南。”大生纱厂的诞生，是张謇迈出其“实业救国”主张的第一步，标志着张謇开始从一个传统士人转变为一个近代企业家。

Founding Dasheng

In 1895, the Qing government began to encourage the private sector to set up new industries amid internal and external crises. At the end of that year, Zhang Zhidong (prominent politician in late Qing) assigned Zhang Jian, the registered squire in Jiangsu, to run the commerce in Jiangsu Province by setting up more yarn and silk factories in line with the local situation. After much consideration, Zhang Jian decided to venture into business. After five years of hard work from 1895 to 1899, Dasheng Cotton Mill, a modernized mill with more than 20,000 spindles, was established in Tangzha Town on the north bank of Yangtze River. On the occasion of the launching of Dasheng Cotton Mill, Weng Tonghe wrote a couplet in celebration, saying "As the spinning machine kicks off, southeast China will have sufficient supply of clothes and quilts." The birth of Dasheng Cotton Mill was the first step taken by Zhang Jian to practice his idea of "saving the country by developing industry", which marked the beginning of his transformation from a traditional scholar to a patriotic entrepreneur.

参与创立民国

1911年10月10日夜晚的武昌，阴雨绵绵，张謇刚登上回南通的“襄阳丸”号江轮，武昌城内的楚望台方向即传来冲天火光。辛亥革命的首义炮火被张謇亲眼目睹。

作为立宪派的领袖人物，张謇一直反对暴力革命，积极推动清廷预备立宪。武昌起义的第三天，张謇到达南京，曾想为清廷做最后的挽救。然而此时，革命的烈火已经蔓延至全国大部分地区，各省纷纷宣布独立，脱离清朝统治。眼见清廷大势已去，张謇政治思想发生转变。他顺应历史潮流，拥护共和，并全力支持革命军进攻南京。

Involvement in Initiating Republicanism

On the rainy night of October 10, 1911, Zhang Jian returned to Nantong by riverboat after finishing his business in Wuchang, Hubei Province. At the moment he stepped onto the riverboat named Xiangyang Maru, raging flames came from the Chuwangtai Armory in Wuchang. The first uprising to overthrow Qing government was witnessed by Zhangjian.

Zhang Jian, as a proponent of constitutionalism, had been committed to transforming Qing government into constitutional government in opposition to violent revolution. On the third day of the Wuchang Uprising, Zhang Jian arrived in Nanjing, trying to do his utmost to save the Qing government. However, by that time, the revolution had spread to most of the country, and many provinces had broken away from the Qing government in succession. As the day of the feudal government had gone, Zhang Jian changed his stand and turned to endorse republicanism by supporting revolutionary army to foray into Nanjing.

位于上海南阳路十号的惜阴堂是张謇好友赵凤昌的居所，在南北和谈期间，这里成为各方代表的汇集地，双方议决的议题，大多先在此讨论。张謇在惜阴堂与各方谋划结束清朝、建立民国的方案，并参与起草了清帝退位诏书。经过赵凤昌、张謇等人从中协调、磋商，南北双方终于达成一致。1912年元旦，中华民国成立。2月12日，清帝逊位。张謇在这一过程中发挥了重要作用。

Xiyintang, located at No.10 Nanyang Road, Shanghai, is the residence of Zhao Fengchang, a bosom friend of Zhang Jian. During peace talks between the Qing government and revolutionaries, the residence became a gathering place for representatives of all parties. Most of the issues concerning the two sides were discussed here first. In Xiyintang, Zhang Jian made plans with other parties to end the Qing Dynasty and establish the Republic of China, and drafted an imperial edict on the abdication of the Qing emperor. Through coordination by Zhao Fengchang, Zhang Jian and others, the two sides finally reached an agreement. The Republic of China was founded on New Year's Day in 1912. On February 12, the Qing emperor abdicated. Zhang Jian played an important role in this process.

出入政坛

1913年10月16日，花甲之年的张謇到达北京，出任袁世凯北洋政府内阁农商总长兼全国水利局总裁。其间，张謇发表了《对于工商部务的政见》等施政宣言，鼓励资本主义发展，规范企业行为，引进资本，实施"棉铁主义"。主持制定"公司条例"等一系列促进国民经济发展的法令；主持拟定一系列发展棉、糖、林、牧的实业计划和方案，和美国红十字会签订导淮借款2000万美元的草约，和美孚石油公司订立3500万美元的借款合同，引进外国技术。这些政策措施，促进了当时民族资本主义的发展。

不久之后，张謇见袁世凯复辟帝制野心高涨，自己的政治理想无法实现，先后辞去农商总长和全国水利局总裁职务，于1915年离开了政坛，将主要精力放在南通地方事业建设上。

Breaking Away from Political Circles

On October 16, 1913, Zhang Jian arrived in Beijing at the age of sixty and took officials posts of the Cabinet Minister of Agriculture and Commerce and the president of the National Water Conservancy Bureau of Beiyang government (1912–1928). During this period, to realize the ideal of national salvation, Zhang Jian published his policy manifestos, such as *Political Opinions on Industry and Commerce Affairs*, encouraging the development of capitalism, regulating the behavior of enterprises and introducing the idea of "Cotton and Iron First". He promulgated *Regulations on Enterprises*, which is the first corporate regulation in modern China. He also presided over an array of plans and programs to develop cotton, sugar, forestry, and animal husbandry.

As Yuan Shikai was determined in restoring monarchy, the political ambition of Zhang Jian was foiled. He resigned the office of Minister of Agriculture and Commerce and president of the National Water Conservancy Bureau, and broke away from political circles in 1915. Later, he focused most of his attention on the development of Nantong.

会须身伴五山灵

1926年8月1日，张謇亲赴江边勘查汛情，连日的高温天气已让他颇感不适，从江堤回来后，张謇就病倒了。此后病情急剧恶化，8月24日夜，张謇不幸去世，走完了73年坎坷又传奇的人生。

张謇出殡那天，“素车白马，四方来会葬的，和地方上人，共有万余人，都步行执绋。凡柩车经过的地方，那沿路观望的乡人，有数十万都屏息嗟叹，注视送别”。“即此粗完一生事，会须身伴五山灵”，这是张謇生前给自己的墓阙写的一副对联，张謇希望自己的灵魂与南通这块热土永远相伴相依。

My Body Will Accompany Five Mountains

On August 1, 1926, Zhang Jian went to the bank of Yangtze River to monitor the flooding, and the hot weather for days had made him feel sick. After coming back from the river bank, Zhang Jian fell ill and his condition deteriorated afterwards. On the night of August 24, Zhang Jian passed away, wrapping up 73 years of rough yet legendary life.

On the day of Zhang Jian's funeral, "more than ten thousand people came on foot to see him off. Wherever the hearse went, people along the road watched and silently lamented his passing." Zhang Jian wrote his own epitaph. It reads, "By now I have finished my life in a rough way, and my body will accompany the five mountains in Nantong." He hoped that his soul would snuggle with the land of Nantong eternally.

敢　为　天　下　先

A Bold Pioneer

开路先锋

1929年，胡适在《南通张季直先生传记》的序言中这样评价张謇：“他独立开辟了无数新路，做了三十年的开路先锋，养活了几百万人，造福于一方，而影响及于全国。”张謇勇于开拓、敢为人先，富有创新精神，在南通开创了诸多全国之最：

大生纺织企业集团——中国最早的民营资本集团；

通海垦牧公司——中国第一个农垦股份制企业；

通州师范学校——中国第一所民立中等师范学校；

南通博物苑——中国人创办的第一座公共博物馆；

南通纺织专门学校——中国第一所纺织高等学校；

伶工学社——中国第一所戏曲学校；

河海工程专门学校——中国第一所水利高等院校；

狼山盲哑学校——中国人自己创办的第一所盲哑学校；

……

Pioneering on Many Fronts

In 1929, Hu Shih said of Zhang Jian in the preface to *Biography of Mr. Zhang Jian in Nantong*, "He has independently opened countless new roads. Being a pioneer for thirty years, he has fed millions of people, benefiting the community and even the whole nation." Zhang Jian dared to be a pioneer and boasted a spirit of innovation, blazing many new trails in Nantong.

Dasheng Textile Enterprise Group – the first private-funded company in China.

Tonghai Reclamation Corporation – the first joint-stock agricultural reclamation enterprise in China.

Tongzhou Normal School – the first civil secondary normal school in China.

Nantong Museum – the first public museum founded by a Chinese.

Nantong Textile Specialized School – the first institution of higher education on textile in China.

The School of Drama – the first drama school in China.

Specialized School on River and Sea Engineering – the first water conservancy institution of higher learning in China.

Wolf Mountain School for the Blind and Mute – the first blind and mute school founded by the Chinese.

……

大生企业集团

——中国第一个大型民营资本集团

张謇是近代“实业救国”思想的代表人物，在“振兴实业”的方略上，张謇进一步提出了“棉尤宜先”的优先发展棉纺织业的主张。1895年底，张謇在通州设立商务局，创办大生纱厂，从此开始将实业救国理想付诸实践。1899年，大生纱厂建成，至1921年历年盈利。1904年大生纱厂生产能力扩大了一倍，1907年建成大生二厂，1921年建成大生三厂，1924年建成大生八厂。至此，大生系统纱锭和布机数分别占全国华商纱厂总数的7.39%和9.8%，是当时全国最大的纺织企业系统。

1901年为建立大生纱厂原料基地，张謇创办通海垦牧公司，开启了苏北沿海垦殖业。后逐步构建以棉纺织业为核心的产业链，发展冶铁、制造、电力、食品、轮船运输业及通讯、金融、商贸、仓储等企业，在南通建立了较为完整的工业体系。至上世纪二十年代初，南通共建成37家企业，在淮南沿海拥有相关的盐垦公司20家，形成一、二、三产业门类齐全、资本额达2483万两白银的大生资本集团，成为当时全国最大的民营资本集团。

Dasheng Enterprise Group

– China's First Large Private Group

Zhang Jian was a representative figure who championed the idea of "revitalizing nation by developing industry". He put forward the "Cotton First Initiative" that prioritized the growth of cotton textile industry. At the end of 1895, Zhang Jian set up the bureau of commerce in Tongzhou and founded Dasheng Cotton Mill, which put his idea of national salvation into practice. In 1899, Dasheng Cotton Mill was set up, and in the next few years eight branches had been built in succession. By 1924, spindles and cloth weaving machines of Dasheng accounted for 7.39% and 9.8% respectively of all cotton mills in China. Back then, it was the largest textile enterprise in China.

In 1901, to supply raw material for Dasheng Cotton Mill, Zhang Jian founded Tonghai Reclamation Company, which was a beginning for extensive reclamation and cultivation in the coastal area of northern Jiangsu Province. Later, Dasheng Group gradually branched into iron smelting, manufacturing, electric power, foodstuff, shipping, communication, finance, trade and commerce, storage, and other areas, forming a complete industrial system. By the early 1920s, Zhang Jian had established 37 enterprises and owned 20 related reclamation companies in the Huainan coast. His property covered primary, secondary, and tertiary industries, valued at 24.83 million taels of silver. Dasheng Group was deemed as the largest private capital group in China at that time.

通海垦牧公司

——中国第一个沿海垦殖公司

大生纱厂开工后，张謇着手在苏北沿海广袤的退化盐场、海涂滩地上实施盐业改良，为大生纱厂开辟原棉生产基地。1901年，张謇设立通海垦牧公司，此为中国第一个沿海垦殖公司，公司的建立历尽艰难，十年后终于初具成效。通海垦牧公司的成功，带动了通海直至苏北沿海一带的垦殖运动，十数年间涌现了40多个农垦公司，吸引了数十万移民北上开垦。通过大规模的废灶兴垦、改良土壤、兴修水利，引进驯化良种，广植棉花，使淮南垦区形成了我国近代最大的产棉区。至1934年，淮南垦区已拥有棉田500多万亩，年产棉花100余万担，两项数据均分别占江苏全省的1/2、中国的1/8，推进了区域现代化的发展。

Tonghai Reclamation Company

– China's First Coastal Reclamation Company

After Dasheng Cotton Mill was opened, Zhang Jian began to work on transforming the deteriorated salt pan and mudflat into the cotton production base for Dasheng Cotton Mill. In 1901, Zhang Jian established the Tonghai Reclamation Company, which was the first coastal reclamation company in China. The company achieved initial success after ten years of operation, which drove the reclamation movement from Nantong to the coastal area of northern Jiangsu Province, and more than 40 reclamation companies emerged afterwards, attracting hundreds of thousands of immigrants to the north for reclamation. Through large-scale reclaiming saltpan for cultivation, soil improvement, water conservancy, introduction of domesticated seeds and extensive cotton planting, the Huainan reclamation area became the largest cotton-producing area in modern China. By 1934, there were more than five million *mu* (about 333333 hectares) of cotton fields in Huainan reclamation area, and produced more than one million quintals of cotton. The area of cotton fields and cotton output accounted for 1/2 of Jiangsu Province and 1/8 of the country respectively, greatly advancing regional modernization.

通州师范学校

——中国第一所民立中等师范学校

张謇是近代“教育救国”思想的代表人物，认为教育对富民强国有着根本性的作用，“图存救亡，舍教育无由”。1902年，张謇本着“立学校则须从小学始，尤须先从师范始”理念，着手兴办学校。次年，通州师范学校开学，这是中国第一所民立中等师范学校。张謇亲任学校总理，为该校题写“坚苦自立，忠实不欺”的校训，并且亲自拟定学校章程，聘请国内外名师，组织留学交流。1905年，张謇又创办了通州女子师范学校。至1926年，两校毕业学生已有1453人。通州师范学校还强化职业教育。从1906年起，张謇在通州师范学校先后附设测绘科、农科、土木工科、蚕科，培养了大批专门技术人才。

Tongzhou Normal School

– China's First Private Secondary Normal School

Zhang Jian was a representative figure that advocated "education for national salvation". He believed that education played a fundamental role in enriching the people and strengthening the country, and that "education is an essential prerequisite for saving the country". In 1902, Zhang Jian started to set up schools based on the idea that "running schools must start from primary schools and especially normal schools". In the following year, Tongzhou Normal School opened; it was the first private secondary normal school in China. Zhang Jian took up the post of the principal and wrote the motto for the school "Being self-reliant and faithful". He drew up the constitution of the school, appointed famous teachers from home and abroad, and arranged exchange program with foreign countries. In 1905, Zhangjian founded Tongzhou Normal School for Women. By 1926, a total of 1453 students had graduated from the two normal schools. Tongzhou Normal School also took vocational education seriously. Starting in 1906, Zhang Jian set up the surveying and mapping department, agriculture department, civil engineering department and sericulture department in the school, which helped to nurture a large array of technical staff.

南通博物苑

——中国第一座公共博物馆

张謇是中国博物馆事业的倡导者。1905年，他在南通创办中国第一座公共博物馆——南通博物苑。张謇亲自指导了馆苑设施的建设，拟订藏品征集启事，广泛搜集中外动植矿物标本、乡里金石文物、先贤遗文，并亲自设计陈列柜架，制定《博物苑观览简章》，形成了切合实际的博物馆工作方针。

南通博物苑是一座园林式的博物馆。苑中广植花草树木、养殖珍禽异兽，与室内展品呼应。各种园林设施点缀其间，体现了馆园结合的独特风貌和中国特色的办馆理念。博物苑西部有濠南别业，为张謇故居，建于1914年，主体建筑是一座四层英式楼房，是我国近代吸收西洋建筑艺术的经典作品，现有张謇生平事迹陈列。南通博物苑现为全国重点文物保护单位。

Nantong Museum

– China's First Public Museum

Zhang Jian was an advocate of Chinese museums, and in 1905 he founded the first public museum in China, Nantong Museum. Zhang Jian directed the construction of the museum facilities in person, and drew up notice for collecting pieces such as Chinese and foreign specimens of animals, plants and minerals, stone and metal relics, and the scripture of past sages. He designed the display cabinets and shelves, formulated the *Brief Guide to the Museum*, and formed practical guidelines for museum work.

Nantong Museum is a garden-style museum. The garden boasts a wide variety of flowers and trees as well as rare birds and animals. The whole property is dotted with various garden facilities. It is the epitome of Chinese cultural institutions that combine garden and museum in one entity. The centerpiece building of Nantong Museum is a four-story English-style construction, which displays Western art of architecture in modern China. Nantong Museum is now a major historical and cultural site protected at the national level.

福海號

江浙渔业公司

——中国第一家渔业公司

1903年，张謇在日本期间参观其博览会“通运馆”时发现日本侵占中国制海权的意图，由此张謇意识到渔业和航政对国家主权的重要性。南通吕四一带盐民多兼营渔业，张謇回国后即筹划组织吕四渔业公司改良渔业，并把这看成是保护海权的关键举措。1904年初，张謇向清廷奏请创办渔业公司，不久即获得商部批准。张謇随即发起招集商股45万两，创办了我国第一家渔业公司——江浙渔业公司，购买了我国第一艘机械拖网渔轮——“福海号”，成为中国机船渔业的发端。江浙渔业公司以保护渔业、保全海权为宗旨开办，开启了中国渔业早期现代化的进程。

Jiangzhe Fishery Company

– China's First Modern Fishery Company in China

In 1903, Zhang Jian detected Japan's intention to intrude on China's command of sea when he visited the exposition in Japan. He proposed that command of sea should not be challenged where fishing was conducted. In Lüsi area of Nantong, many residents made salt from seawater while fishing for a living. Zhang Jian worked on organizing Lüsi Fishery Company upon returning to Nantong, making it a key move to safeguard command of sea. In early 1904, Zhang Jian appealed to the Qing government for founding a fishery company. His appeal was approved soon by the Ministry of Commerce. Zhang Jian then raised 450,000 taels of silver to found Jiangzhe Fishery Company, the first modern fishing company in China, and purchased the first mechanical fishing trawler "Fuhai". For the purpose of protecting the fishing industry and safeguarding command of sea, Jiangzhe Fishery Company kicked off early-stage modernization of Chinese fishery.

江苏省立水产学校

——中国第一所水产高等院校

张謇在创办渔业公司的同时，向清廷奏请设立水产、商船学校。1905年，江浙渔业公司附近的360余亩土地获准用于水产、商船学校的规划用地，并先在此办了一所渔业小学。1909年，张謇在江苏省咨议局议长任上再次倡议建水产学校，直至民国建立后，才由江苏省临时议会于1912年正式批准，成立江苏省立水产学校，俗称吴淞水产学校。学校由黄炎培统筹规划、组织实施。学校设有渔捞、制造、养殖等科，后增设航海专科和远洋渔业专科。该校是当今海洋领域的著名高校——上海海洋大学的前身。

Jiangsu Provincial Aquatic School

– China's First Aquatic Institution of Higher Education

While founding fishery companies, Zhang Jian applied to the Qing government for setting up aquatic school and merchant marine academy. In 1905, he was allowed to use over 24-hectare land near Jiangzhe Fishery Company for the planning of aquatic school and merchant marine academy. In 1909, Zhang Jian as speaker of Jiangsu Provincial Advisory Bureau proposed to build aquatic schools for the second time. However, it was until 1912 that the aquatic school was approved by the Provisional Assembly of Jiangsu Province. The provincial aquatic school was commonly known as Wusong Aquatic School, which was planned and organized by Huang Yanpei. Fishing, manufacturing and breeding departments were set up in the school. Later, navigation and ocean fishery specialties were added. The school was later transformed into Shanghai Ocean University, a well-known university in the ocean field.

吴淞商船学校

——中国第一所航海高等院校

吴淞商船学校的前身为清邮传部上海高等实业学堂的船政科，1911年船政科从中分区分出，成立了邮传部高等商船学堂。1912年改由国民政府交通部直辖，改名吴淞商船学校。

此前的1905年，张謇曾筹资在吴淞筹建商船学校，因故未果。此次吴淞商船学校筹建时，张謇将当年学校的规划用地及所筹资金6万元拨付该校，并为学校推荐了萨镇冰担任校长。1915年，吴淞商船学校停办。其后，张謇曾多次致函要求续办商船学校。1929年该校改为交通部吴淞商船专科学校正式复校，为当今名校大连海事大学和上海海事大学的前身。

Wusong Merchant Marine School

– China's First Higher Education Institution for Navigation

The predecessor of Wusong Merchant Marine School was the shipping department of Shanghai Higher Industrial College of the Ministry of Post and Communications in the Qing government. In 1911, the shipping department was separated from its subdivision and the Higher Merchant Marine College of the Ministry of Post and Communications was established. In 1912, it was directly governed by the Ministry of Communications of the Republic of China and renamed Wusong Merchant Marine School.

Previously, in 1905, Zhang Jian had raised funds to purchase land to build a merchant marine school in Wusong, but failed. When Wusong Merchant Marine School was under preparation, Zhang Jian allocated the planned land and 60,000-yuan fund raised before. He also recommended Sa Zhenbing to act as the president of the school. However, in 1915, Wusong Merchant Marine School was closed. After the closure, Zhang Jian wrote for many times to request re-opening of the merchant marine school. Finally in 1929, the school was resumed and renamed Wusong Merchant Marine College affiliated to Ministry of Communications. It is the predecessor of Dalian Maritime University and Shanghai Maritime University.

河海工程专门学校

——中国第一所水利专业高等学校

1913年4月，张謇被国民政府任为导淮局督办。12月，导淮局升为全国水利局，张謇作为北洋政府实业总长兼任全国水利局总裁。张謇任职后发表了《条议疏浚全国水利呈》，其中提出了设立河海工程专门学校的计划。为节省开办费用，尽快招生开学，张謇借用原江苏省咨议局的房屋作为校舍，聘请留美归来的许肇南为校主任（1919年改称校长），聘请时任江苏省教育司长的黄炎培为学校筹备主任，并且聘任了一批从欧美著名大学学成归国的专家学者任教。在张謇精心推动下，1915年3月15日，河海工程专门学校正式开学，张謇专程赶到南京参加典礼。这是我国历史上第一所培养水利技术专门人才的高等学府。

Hohai Engineering Specialized School

– China's First Higher Education School Specializing in Water Conservancy

In April 1913, Zhang Jian was appointed as the supervisor of the Bureau for Treating Huai River. In December that year, the Bureau was upgraded to the National Water Conservancy Bureau, and Zhang Jian acted as Minister of Industry and Commerce and concurrently president of National Water Conservancy Bureau in Beiyang Government. Zhang Jian published the *Report on Dredging Waterway and Water Conservancy*, in which he proposed the plan of establishing a special school for river and sea engineering. Zhang Jian borrowed the house of the former Jiangsu Provincial Advisory Bureau to use as the school building, and hired Xu Zhaonan who returned from the United States as president. He also appointed Huang Yanpei, the then the director of education department of Jiangsu Province, as the preparatory director of the school, and appointed a group of experts and scholars who returned from Europe and the Unites States as teachers. Under the promotion of Zhang Jian, the Hohai Engineering Special School was officially opened on March 15, 1915. This is the first institution of higher education in the history of China to cultivate specialized talents in water conservancy.

军山气象台

——中国第一座气象台

张謇认为“气象不明，不足以完全自治”。早在1906年，张謇即在南通博物苑建“测候室”，配备仪器，对南通气候进行观察记录。张謇在担任北洋政府农商总长兼水利局总裁期间，更重视气象对农林、水利的重要意义，于1914年建立部属的测候总所，通令各省农业机关设立气象测候分所26处，这是全国普遍设立农业气象站的开端。1913年，张謇开始筹建军山气象台，并派青年学生刘渭清赴徐家汇气象台学习，所有仪器由上海徐家汇观象台代购。军山气象台于1917年1月1日正式建成，是我国第一所气象台，张謇亲任总理。该台记录、编印的气象季报、年报及年报辑要中英文对照本，分送国内与世界各国气象台及有关机关百余处，在国际上有相当声誉，曾被列入英国出版的国际气象台名册中。

Junshan Observatory

– China's First Observatory

Zhang Jian believed that "meteorology is necessary for self-governance". As early as 1906, Zhang Jian built a "weather monitoring room" in the Nantong Museum, equipped with instruments to observe and record the climate of Nantong. While holding the post of the Minister of Industry and Commerce and the president of National Water Conservancy Bureau in the Beiyang Government, Zhang Jian attached more importance to meteorology and considered it as a key factor for developing agriculture, forestry and water conservancy. He established a general station of weather monitoring at the ministerial level, and directed all agricultural organs at the provincial level to set up 26 branches of weather monitoring, which marked the beginning of building agrometeorological stations across the country. In 1913, Zhang Jian prepared to set up Junshan Observatory. He sent Liu Weiqing, a young student, to study at Xujiahui Observatory in Shanghai, and entrusted Xujiahui Observatory to purchase all instruments needed. On January 1, 1917, Junshan Meteorological Observatory was officially completed, which was the first observatory in China's history.

南通纺织专门学校

——中国第一所纺织专业高等学校

为满足棉纺织工业对专业技术人才的需求，张謇于1912年创办了纺织染传习所，次年定名“南通纺织专门学校”，这是中国第一所纺织专业高等学校。张謇为该校亲自题写“忠实不欺，力求精进”的校训，又撰写《纺织专门学校旨趣书》，希望通过纺织人才的培养，使中国的纺织工业尽快结束“延欧人以司其命”的现状，早日有“自树立之一日”。纺织专门学校学制为本科、预科两种，采用美国费城纺织学校的课程内容，强调“手脑并用”“实地之经验”。至1917年，已有本科毕业生两届，约50多人，分赴全国各纺织厂服务。1921年，该校毕业生主持完成了大生三厂全部纺织新机的排车设计与安装工程。1927年改称“南通纺织大学”。南通纺织专门学校是培养中国纺织专业人才的摇篮，中国纺织行业从此打破了洋人对纺织技术的垄断。至1952年院系调整前，该校共培养了1700余名纺织科技人才，约占全国纺织科技人才总数的1/4，分布于全国主要纺织企业、纺织院校和科研、管理机构。

Nantong Textile Specialized School

– China's First Textile Specialized Higher Education School

To meet the demand for professional, technical talents in the cotton textile industry, Zhang Jian founded the Training Institute for Textile Dyeing in 1912 and changed its name to "Nantong Textile Specialized School" in the following year, which was the first of its kind in China. Zhang Jian inscribed the school motto "Be faithful and not deceitful, striving for perfection" and wrote *Aims of Textile Specialized School*, hoping that through the cultivation of textile talents, China's textile industry would end the status quo of "depending on the West" and become self-reliant as soon as possible. The school introduced courses from the Philadelphia Textile School, emphasizing "using both mind and hands" and "field experience". By 1917, there were two classes of 50 graduates, who went to serve in various textile factories in China. In 1921, the graduates presided over the design and installation of all the new textile machines in the Dasheng Mill III . In 1927, the school was renamed Nantong Textile University. Nantong Textile Specialized School is a cradle for nurturing specialized talents in textile, and it contributed to breaking the monopoly of the foreigners in textile technology. By 1952, the school had trained more than 1,700 students in textile technology, accounting for about 1/4 of the total number of textile professionals in China. Its graduates worked in major textile enterprises, textile colleges and research institutions across the country.

伶工学社

——中国第一所戏剧学校

张謇说："教育以通俗为最普及，通俗教育以戏剧为易观感。"为此，张謇聘请戏剧艺术家欧阳予倩来南通筹建戏剧学校，并于1919年建成伶工学社，由欧阳予倩任主任，主持校务工作，其子张孝若任社长，这是全国最早的新型戏剧学校。建成开学后，张謇还亲自讲授修身课，批阅学生书法习作，协助国文教材篇目选编。至1926年停办时，伶工学社共培养了戏剧专业人才60多人，在戏剧教育和艺术创新方面作了许多尝试，在我国戏剧史上享有特殊地位。

1919年，张謇还建成了一座全国一流的新型剧场——更俗剧场。剧场实施了一系列移风易俗的新的管理制度，曾邀请著名京剧表演艺术家梅兰芳到南通与欧阳予倩同台演出。

Linggong Academy

– China's First Drama School

Zhang Jian believed that drama as the main form of popular culture had a more direct role in promoting social civilization. For this reason, Zhang Jian hired the theater artist Ouyang Yuqian to build a drama school in Nantong, and in 1919, he built the Linggong Academy, with Ouyang Yuqian as the director and his son Zhang Xiaoruo as the president. The academy is the earliest new-style drama school in China. Zhang Jian taught the class how to cultivate moral character, reviewed the calligraphy work of students, and assisted in the selection and compilation of the Chinese textbook. By 1926, when the school was closed, it had trained more than 60 theater professionals and made many breakthroughs in theater education and artistic innovation, which enjoyed a special status in the history of Chinese theater.

In 1919, Zhang Jian built a national first-class new-style theater, the Gengsu Theater (Gengsu means changing prevailing habits and customs). The theater implemented new management system to change customs and traditions, and invited artist Mei Lanfang, famous master of Beijing opera, to perform on the same stage with Ouyang Yuqian in Nantong.

師范学校

中国第一个实施全境地理测绘的地区

张謇认识到城市发展需要建立在科学规划的基础之上，而规划的基础是测绘。他说："欲求自治，则必自有舆图始，欲有舆图，则必自测绘始"，"建设之先须规划，规划之先须测绘"，"建设之规划求其当，规划之测绘求其详，循序以进"。1906年7月，张謇在通州师范学校附设了测绘科，以培养测绘人才。1908年1月，测绘科43名学生毕业。张謇以测绘科毕业生为基本队伍，建立了通州测绘局，并自任局长，开始对南通进行地理测绘。从1908—1911年，测绘面积为南通全境7435方里，共测图791幅，绘图865幅，比例尺从1：5000到1：250000共6种。自1915年8月起的两年间，测绘局又进行了一次较大规模的全境水利测绘，共测图345幅，绘图401幅，比例尺均为1：5000。

The First City in the Country to Implement Territory-wide Geographic Mapping

Zhang Jian realized that urban development must be based on scientific planning, and the basis of planning is surveying and mapping. He said, "To realize self-governance, we must rely on maps. Drawing maps must start from surveying... All constructions shall begin with planning, and planning should begin with surveying and mapping." In July 1906, Zhang Jian set up a surveying and mapping department in Tongzhou Normal School to cultivate surveying and mapping talents. Forty-three students graduated from the surveying and mapping department in January 1908. With these graduates as the initial members, Zhang Jian established Tongzhou Surveying and Mapping Bureau. As its director, Zhang Jian conducted geographic surveying and mapping of Nantong. From 1908 to 1911, 7435 square *li* (about 1858 square kilometers) of the whole Nantong was surveyed and mapped. The scale of the maps ranged from 1:5000 to 1:250000. In two years starting from August 1915, the Surveying and Mapping Bureau carried out another large-scale waterway mapping, yielding 345 maps and 401 drawings, all at a scale of 1:5000.

中国第一个的普及义务教育的县

通州师范学校建成后，张謇于1904年设立“通州五属学务处”，作为推广新式教育的办事机构，谋划五属（通州、静海、海门、如皋、泰兴）共同筹建各地的初等和高等小学。

为方便学生就近入学，在亲自步行测算的基础上，从1908年起，张謇着手制定和实施每16平方里设立一所小学分区布局的规划。南通由此开始逐步从传统教育体制向近代教育体制转变。

1911年，张謇主持制定了州（县）级地方普及4年义务教育的规划，并努力推进实施。至1926年，南通县已建有初级小学329所，在校学生1.92万人；完全小学计21所，在校学生4013人。南通成为中国第一个普及4年制义务教育的县。

The First County in the Country to Achieve Universal Compulsory Education

After establishing Tongzhou Normal School, Zhang Jian set up the Tongzhou Office for School Affairs in Five Areas in 1904 to promote the new education, and planned to build primary schools in the five areas of Nantong (Tongzhou, Jinghai, Haimen, Rugao and Taixing).

To make students go to the nearest school, Zhang Jian measured the distance himself by walking. From 1908 onwards, he started to formulate and implement the plan of building one elementary school for every four square kilometers.

In 1911, Zhang Jian presided over the plan of universal 4-year compulsory education at the municipal (county) level and made great efforts to put it into effect. By 1926, there were 19,200 students in 329 elementary schools and 4,013 students in 21 primary schools with the full six grades. Nantong became the first county in China to spread 4-year compulsory education extensively.

“中国近代第一城”

《中国大百科全书 · 建筑 · 园林 · 城市规划卷》（1988年版）“城市规划”导论对南通的近代城市规划给予很高评价：鸦片战争后，“中国也出现了新的城市规划学。……在实践方面，特别值得一提的是南通的城市规划和建设。1895—1925年，在中国实业家张謇推动下，南通为了发展近代工业和航运，开辟了新工业区和港区，建立了多核心的城镇体系，旧城内辟市场、兴学校、建博物馆、修道路，进行了近代市政建设。”

2002年，中国城市规划的权威、两院院士吴良镛通过对南通与西方同时代城市和近代中国同时期城市的对比，认为张謇经营的南通在城市建设及其理论方面更具典型性和相对完整性，南通堪称“中国近代第一城”。

The Pioneering City in Modern China

The *Encyclopedia of China – Architecture, Landscape Garden and Urban Planning* (1988 Edition) speaks highly of Nantong's modern urban planning, "After the Opium War, the new urban planning science emerged in China... In practice, Nantong's urban planning and construction is particularly noteworthy. From 1895 to 1925, facilitated by the Chinese industrialist Zhang Jian, Nantong opened new industrial and port areas, established a multi-core town system, and built schools, museums, roads, and such facilities to develop modern industry and shipping."

In 2002, Wu Liangyong, an authority on urban planning in China and a member of the Chinese Academy of Sciences and Chinese Academy of Engineering, compared Nantong with its western contemporaries and modern Chinese cities of the same period. He concluded that Nantong run by Zhang Jian was more typical and relatively complete in terms of urban construction, and Nantong can be called "the pioneering city in modern China".

国　家　兴　亡

匹　夫　有　责

Everyone Has a Stake
in the Rise and Fall of the Nation

天下興亡匹夫有責

以天下为己任

早在同治十三年（1874）的夏天，张謇随调任江宁发审局的孙云锦到淮安视察，他发现学问不仅仅限于书本，还应在实际事务中获得，并留下了“船山不是一经儒”等诗句，表明他有继承明末清初经世致用思想的强烈愿望。

张謇自幼对民间疾苦耳濡目染，加上饱读诗书，因此特别推崇黄宗羲、顾炎武等人的思想。他曾说：“亭林匹夫兴亡有责之言，黎洲原臣视民水火之义，故常闻之而识之矣。凡夫可以鼓新气、祓旧俗、保种类、明圣言之事，无不坚牢矢愿奋然为之，以为是天下之大命，吾人之职业也。”面对近代中国民不聊生的现实，张謇“在商仍向儒”，甘以天下为己任，通过兴实业、办教育、广慈善，为改善民生而不懈努力。

Taking the Destiny of the Country as His Own Responsibility

In the summer of 1874, Zhang Jian went to Huai'an for inspection. What he saw on the journey had produced profound impression on him that knowledge should not only be obtained from books but also from activities. He left behind such poetic lines as "Wang Fuzhi (a scholar of Ming-Qing transition) is by no means a scholar who passes on Confucianism mechanically".

Zhang Jian had witnessed sufferings inflicted on the people. As he was well-read, he advocated the ideas of Huang Zongxi and Gu Yanwu (scholar and writer of the Ming-Qing transition). He once said, "I live by the earnest teachings of past sages like Gu Yanwu and Huang Zongxi that everyone should be concerned about the country's fate and people's sufferings. Mortal men like me are duty-bound to boost our morale, reform old customs, and uphold the teachings of past sages." Zhang Jian honored his words. He worked hard to develop industries while boosting education and charity, making unremitting efforts to improve the well-being of people.

知恥後勇
是誰亟續責和篇
遺恨長留乙未年
第一游人須記取
春帆樓上馬關前
目睹這一給中國帶來巨大屈辱的小樓
張謇
民興賦詩
民族復興
日清講和紀念館

愤笔春帆楼

《马关条约》的签订使张謇悲愤不已。一方面，张謇对日本的侵华行径一贯痛恨；另一方面，他对明治维新以后学习西方迅速富强的日本颇为倾服，一直有想去日本考察的愿望。

1903年5月21日至7月29日，张謇对日本进行了为期70天的考察。赴日期间，张謇除重点参加大阪博览会外，还考察了日本的教育机构、农工商企业等。此期间，张謇还专程前往《马关条约》签订地春帆楼，探访这一给中华民族带来巨大屈辱的小楼。虽已事过八载，但张謇愤慨不减，当即赋诗一首："是谁亟续贵和篇，遗恨长留乙未年。第一游人须记取，春帆楼上马关前。"张謇知耻而后勇，勇于向对手学习，回国以后，他把在日本学到的经验用于他的救国实践。

Lamenting at Shunpanro

The signing of the *Treaty of Shimonoseki* filled Zhang Jian with grief and indignation. Harboring enormous hatred towards Japan's invasion of China, Zhang Jian was nonetheless impressed by Japan, which had learned from the West to become rich and strong after the Meiji Restoration, and he had the desire to visit Japan.

From May 21 to July 29, 1903, Zhang Jian made a 70-day visit to Japan. Besides attending the Osaka Exposition, he visited Japanese educational institutions and agricultural and industrial enterprises. During this period, Zhang Jian also made a special trip to Shunpanro where the humiliating *Treaty of Shimonoseki* was signed. Although eight years had passed, his indignation was not diminished, and he composed a poem to express his grief, "Making compromises for peace settlement left eternal regret. Any visitor must not forget the humiliation of *Shimonoseki Treaty* at Shunpanro". Knowing what is shameful is akin to bravery. After returning home, Zhang Jian applied what he learned in Japan in his practice of saving the country.

百世以公为公

1921年，张謇在南通城南修建曹公祠，纪念明代抗倭英雄曹顶。曹顶是明嘉靖年间通州余西场盐民，倭寇进犯通州时，他应募入伍，在与抗倭的战斗中壮烈牺牲。建祠之时，张謇题联：“匹夫犹耻国非国，百世以为公可公”“北郭留名单家店，南山增气曹公坟”，并撰写《重修曹公祠碑》，歌颂曹顶抗击倭寇的光荣事迹，告诫国人要警惕日本侵略，勿忘甲午战败之耻。除了重修曹公祠外，张謇还重建过文天祥渡海亭，作《重建宋文忠烈公渡海亭记》，弘扬文天祥的爱国忠心和民族气节。张謇把家国情怀融入进历史遗迹中，通过保护修缮这些历史遗迹，发挥其爱国主义教育的功能。

Our Admiration for Cao Ding Passes on from Generation to Generation

In 1921, Zhang Jian built the Cao Ding Shrine in the south of Nantong City to honor Cao Ding, a hero of the Ming Dynasty who fought against the Japanese. When the Japanese invaded Tongzhou, Cao Ding was recruited into the army and died in the battle against the Japanese pirates. When the shrine was completed, Zhang Jian inscribed the couplets “Even coarse fellow is ashamed of the ruined country; our admiration for Cao Ding passes on from generation to generation”, “Glorious memory of you is left in Shanjiadian (where Cao Ding fought to death); our morale is boosted by this shrine”. He also wrote *Restoration of Cao Ding’s Shrine* to extol Cao Ding’s glorious deeds of fighting against Japanese invaders and warning the nation to be vigilant against Japanese invasion. In addition to restoring Cao Ding Shrine, Zhang Jian rebuilt Wen Tianxiang Memorial Pavilion (Wen Tianxiang is a hero resisting Mongol invasion in Song Dynasty), and wrote *The Record of Rebuilding Wen Zhongxiang Memorial Pavilion* to publicize Wen Tianxiang’s loyalty and integrity. Zhang Jian invested his patriotism in the historical relics and through preserving and restoring these historical relics, people’s awareness of patriotism was heightened.

國何為而須教育教育者期人民知有國而已小必期其愛鄉大必期其愛國愛鄉則必期鄉治愛國則必期國治

唤醒民众爱国精神

晚清社会中，民众对乡土观念，远重于国家观念。近代以来，民族国家观念在知识分子中觉醒。唤醒普通民众国家观念和爱国精神是张謇教育理念中的首要内容。张謇说，“国何为而须教育？教育者，期人民知有国而已”，通过教育激发国民的责任和担当。张謇把爱国和爱乡的教育结合起来，认为“小必期其爱乡，大必期其爱国。爱乡则必期乡治，爱国则必期国治”。在激发民众爱国强国意识的同时，他希望南通人民把对爱乡的情感落实在“地方自治”的行动上。在深受列强欺辱的近代，张謇弘扬爱国主义、树立民族精神，努力塑造南通新的城市精神。

Raising Patriotism among the People

In the late Qing society, people were more attached to their hometown than the nation. In modern times, the awareness of nation and state developed among intellectuals. To awaken the national awareness and patriotic spirit among the general public was the first and foremost part of Zhang Jian's philosophy for developing education. Zhang Jian remarked, "What is the need of education for the country? Education is for the people to know that we all belong to a country." It is through education that the responsibility and commitment of the people are stimulated. Zhang Jian combined the education of patriotism with people's affection towards hometown. He said, "In narrow sense, everyone is expected to love his hometown. In broad sense, everyone is expected to love his country. Those who love their hometown anticipate well-governed hometown, and those who love their country anticipate a well-ruled country." While raising the people's awareness of patriotism, Zhang Jian hoped that the people of Nantong could translate their affection towards hometown into practices of "self-governance at local level". In the modern era, when China was deeply humiliated by the imperial powers, patriotism and national spirit were main elements in the spirit of Nantong city.

强　毅　之　力
利　民　之　智

Fighting with an Indomitable Will to Enlighten the People

强毅之力行其志

“状元办厂”历尽艰难。在大生纱厂创办初期，张謇面临的首要问题便是集股筹资，最初议定由“通沪六董”共同出资集股，但沪董迟疑观望，不愿出资，大生不得不从最初的商办改变为“绅领商办”。集股问题基本解决了以后，1897年张謇开始动工建造工厂，各项开支耗费巨大，大生又陷入捉襟见肘的窘境。地方官僚对张謇的办厂行为也多番阻挠。然而，张謇办厂的意志是坚定的，困难并没有让其退缩。大生纱厂几度山穷水尽，又几度起死回生，终于在1899年5月23日正式开车。在经历种种磨难之后，大生纱厂进入了一个相对顺利的发展期，可谓“否极泰来”。

Being Resolute in Fulfilling His Aspiration

Zhang Jian went through many hardships in running factories. At the early stage of founding Dasheng Cotton Mill, the first problem encountered was raising money. Initially, it was agreed that “the six directors of Nantong and Shanghai” would jointly raise fund, but the directors of Shanghai were hesitant and unwilling to contribute, so Dasheng had to change from the initial commercial operation to “commercial operation led by squire”. Zhang Jian started to build the factory in 1897, and the expenses were so huge that Dasheng was again strapped for cash. The local bureaucrats also obstructed factory operation. However, Zhang Jian’s will to run the factory was firm and the difficulties did not deter him. He pulled the cotton mill back from the brink for several times, and finally the mill was opened on May 23, 1899. Despite all the setbacks, Dasheng Cotton Mill developed quite smoothly after its launching, which could be summarized by Chinese saying “out of worst misfortune comes fortune”.

棉铁主义

1895年《马关条约》签订以后，外商纷纷在华投资设厂，不仅疯狂地掠夺中国的资源，也限制了中国民族工商业的发展。张謇见微知著，在《代鄂督条陈立国自强疏》中指出，洋商在“内地开机器厂”，是夺“小民一线生机”。张謇研究了清光绪、宣统年间的海关贸易册后，发现当时进口的最大宗商品是棉纺织品，其次是钢铁，“就各项实业而言，最为吾所主张者为棉、铁二项，以其于近世界中为必不可少之物也”，进而提出了“棉铁主义”“棉宜优先”战略。他认为，与民生最为相关的产业“无过于纺织，纺织中最适于中国普通用者惟棉”，“而我国铁矿蕴藏丰富，如能利用，岁可得数千万”，因此为挽回利权，保护民生，中国必须先行“推广棉地、纺织厂”及“开放铁矿、扩张制铁厂”，发展棉铁两业，就“可以操经济界之全权”。大生纱厂和资生铁厂的创办，便是张謇“棉铁主义”经济思想的具体实践。

Cotton and Iron First

After the signing of the *Treaty of Shimonoseki* in 1895, foreign businesses began to invest in China, which not only plundered China's resources, but also restricted the development of national industry and commerce. Zhang Jian pointed out in the *Commentary on Strengthening the Nation* that foreign-run mechanized factories in China were taking means of livelihood away from ordinary people. After studying the customs trade books of Qing Dynasty, Zhang Jian found that the commodity imported most at that time was cotton and textile, followed by iron and steel. "As far as industries are concerned, the two items I advocate most are cotton and iron, which are essential in the today's world." He then proposed the "cotton and iron first" and "cotton takes precedence" initiatives. He believed that the industry closest to people's livelihood was the textile industry, and the most suitable textile material for general use in China was cotton. China was rich in iron ore, which could produce tens of millions profits in a year. Therefore, to protect people's livelihood, China must "promote cotton cultivation and textile factories" and "open iron mines and expand iron works". By developing the cotton textile and iron industries, China can take its economy under control. The establishment of Dasheng Cotton Mill and Zisheng Iron Works were the practices of Zhang Jian's economic idea of "cotton and iron first".

土产外销

清代，南通农民生产的土布已远销东北，因其粗厚结实，深受东北民众欢迎，形成“关庄布”业。但因产量有限，不能满足需求。大生纱厂创办后，乡民逐渐改用机制棉纱织布，产量和质量努力提升，外销数量大增。张謇努力推动“关庄布”的销售，形成“棉花——棉纱——棉布”的土产外销链。

“关庄布”的传统运输路线以陆道运输为主。陆道运输从江苏、山东北上进入河北，再经山海关抵达锦州等东北集散地。这条线路长约1500千米，厘卡无数，风险大周期长。为此，张謇通盘筹划，依靠宁波商船“号帮”，采用“北洋线”水道将“关庄布”销往东北市场，即从南通沿江港口向东经长江进入吴淞口，沿海路向北直抵营口、牛庄等集散地。这种“土产外销”经营谋略大获成功，大大促进了南通土布业的发展，仅1903—1904年间，南通“关庄布”销往东北市场的数量总计达到600多万匹。

Selling Local Products to the Market Outside of Nantong

After the establishment of Dasheng Cotton Mill, the output of machine-made cotton cloth was improved, and the quantity sold to the market outside of Nantong increased greatly. Zhang Jian worked hard to promote the sales of handwoven cloth and the out-bound sales chain of cotton, cotton yarn and cotton cloth formed.

The traditional transport route of handwoven cloth was mainly by land. The land transport went north from Jiangsu and Shandong into Hebei, and then arrived at the northeast distribution center such as Jinzhou through Shanhai Pass. This route was about 1500 kilometers long with countless check posts, featuring long cycle and great risks. For this reason, Zhang Jian made a comprehensive arrangement and relied on Ningbo merchant fleets to sell "handwoven cloth" to the northeast market by waterway. That means transporting goods from Nantong river port to Wusong port of Shanghai through the Yangtze River, and then travelling north to distribution centers in Northeast China by sea. In 1903 and 1904, a total of over 6 million bolts of "handwoven cloth" had been sold to the northeast market.

信幸相连

诚信与幸运有时总是相伴相连。1899年大生纱厂正式开车以后，为了早日出纱，取信于人，张謇将价值8万两的棉花转运上海变卖，但仍不能解决资金短缺的困难。在上海，他再次四处求援无果，这让他感到百计俱穷，心力交瘁。最后连回家的旅费都成了问题，只得卖字筹措。正当他一筹莫展之际，他的助手沈燮均建议"尽花纺纱，卖纱收花，更续自转，至不能有花纺纱，则停车闭厂，以还股东"。张謇采纳其建议，做好了"至无花可纺时，停车闭厂"的最坏打算，毅然将纱锭运转起来。幸运的是，这时市场上纱价上涨，大生纱厂当年获纯利3.8万余两。有了利润之后，张謇及时清理亏欠，使大生企业保持着良好信誉，维持着正常运转。后来的经营中，张謇也始终强调纱厂的借款要有借有还，即使在资金周转困难时刻，也始终把诚信摆在首位。

Fortune Always Comes with Integrity

After the official opening of Dasheng Cotton Mill in 1899, Zhang Jian sold off 80,000 taels worth of cotton in Shanghai to raise fund, but the factory was still capital-strapped. He then asked for help in Shanghai to no avail, which made him feel physically and mentally exhausted. In the end, he even had no money left for travelling back home, and was reduced to selling his calligraphy works. When he was at his wit's end, his assistant Shen Xiejun suggested that "we put all the cotton we have into making yarn, and then sell yarn to buy more cotton, thus forming a cycle." Zhang Jian took the advice and put all the spindles into operation, selling yarn and collecting cotton at the same time. He even made the worst plan of "closing the factory when there was no cotton to spin". Fortunately, the market price of yarn increased and Dasheng Cotton mill made a net profit of more than 38,000 taels that year. With the profit, Zhang Jian paid back debts in time, so that Dasheng could maintain good reputation and normal operation. Later on, Zhang Jian always emphasized that the loans of the factory should be repaid in time, and he always put integrity in the first place even when faced with tight cash flow.

让利育商

1913年春初开盘时，大生纱厂每箱纱价150元，售出1万余箱，获得丰厚利润。但不久之后的国民党领导人宋教仁遇刺，紧接着“二次革命”爆发，动荡的政局大大影响了棉纱市场的正常运营。此时，张謇审时度势，“为养成商贾活势计，不得不予扶持，略贬盘价”，每箱以142元的价格让利出售，共售出5千余箱，获得了一定利润。正是张謇善于经营，适度让利，与商户建立了牢固的互信合作关系，从而使大生企业稳住了发展根基。1913年，张謇在大生纱厂第十五届说略中称“出纱视昔为多，开支视前为节，而赢利又视上届为优”。这一年，大生企业利润增至286821两，利润率高达33.13%。

Cutting Price in Favor of Other Merchants

At the early spring of 1913, Dasheng Cotton Mill sold more than 10,000 boxes of yarn at 150 yuan per box and made a huge profit. Shortly afterward, Song Jiaoren, the leader of the Nationalist Party, was assassinated and the Second Revolution against Yuan Shikai and the Northern Warlords erupted. Turbulent political situation exerted negative influence on the market of cotton yarn. Zhang Jian sized up the situation and “for the sake of nourishing the merchants, we had to support them and slightly depreciate the price”, selling yarn at the price of 142 yuan per box. In 1913, Zhang Jian recorded in the 15th report of Dasheng Cotton Mill that “the output of yarn was larger than before, the expenses were lower, and the profit was higher.” In that year, the profit of Dasheng increased to 286,821 taels of silver, and the profit rate was as high as 33.13%.

与海相磨

南通沿海一带，自古是盐场。到清末，随着海岸线不断东移，原先的盐场逐渐退化为荒滩，失去了产盐的功能。为了开发利用这片荒滩，20世纪初，张謇提出“废灶兴垦”方针，筹划在沿海滩涂建立垦牧公司，“广植棉产，以厚纱厂自助之力”。

1901年，通海垦牧公司创办。创办垦牧公司，很多困难都与“海”有关，曾任垦牧公司协理的江知源讲过：“要随时随事用心力与海相磨，能磨，则终身是我强而海弱也。”张謇和江知源等带领南通人民在黄海滩涂上“与海相磨”，进行了一系列艰辛的实践。他们收购土地，确定了沿海滩涂的产权问题；招收移民，以优厚的条件吸引劳动力前来开发；修筑海堤，改变围垦土地的盐碱性。垦牧公司所在地定名“海复镇”，便是取“沧海复桑田”之意。

Grappling with the Sea

The coastal area of Nantong has been a salt farm since ancient times. In the late Qing Dynasty, as the coastline kept moving eastward, the original salt field gradually degenerated into barren beaches and lost its function of producing salt. In the early 20th century, Zhang Jian took the lead in proposing "reclaiming deserted salt field" and planned to establish a reclamation company in the coastal mudflats to "plant cotton extensively so as to facilitate the development of the cotton mill".

In 1901, Tonghai Reclamation Company was founded. Most of the difficulties encountered during founding the company were about the sea. Jiang Zhiyuan, associate manager of the company said, "We should grapple with the sea with our mind and strength at any time and at any place, and we will definitely prevail over the sea." Together with Jiang Zhiyuan, Zhang Jian led the people of Nantong to "fight with the sea" on the Yellow Sea mudflats and carried out a series of arduous practices. They purchased land to make the property rights of the coastal mudflats clear, attracted immigrants with excellent payment to work on the mudflats, and built seawalls to improve saline-alkali soil of the reclaimed land. The location of the company was named "Haifu Town" in the sense of "the reclaimed mudflat turned farming land". After the successful establishment of the company, the coastal mudflats in northern Jiangsu ushered in a boom of development, and "the deserted beaches of the past became fertile fields".

“公司＋农户”的创举

通海垦牧公司是中国第一家农垦股份制公司。张謇从实际出发，对原崇明、海门一带普遍采用的“崇划制”的土地经营方式进行改造，创新建立“公司+农户”的经营模式，获得了成功。

通海垦牧公司通过发行股票以筹集资金，公司的大政方针由董事会决定，土地所有者凭股票向公司支取利润，从而实现了土地所有权和经营权的分离。

垦牧公司的绝大部分耕地出租给农户耕种，每年的租额采取“议租”方式确定，农户与公司按四六分成。这种租佃制的实行，有利于通海垦牧公司统筹全局，完成单个小农家庭无法单独完成的农田水利基本建设、农业技术推广等生产组织功能。

A Remarkable Creation of "Company plus Farmers"

Tonghai Reclamation Company is the first joint-stock agricultural company in China. In view of actual situation, Zhang Jian reformed the land management mode commonly used in Chongming and Haimen to create business model of "company plus farmers", which achieved great success.

The company raised money through issuing stocks and made general policies through decisions by the board of directors. The landowners, as shareholders, received dividends from the company with their shares, which separated land ownership and management rights.

Most of the farming land of the reclamation company was leased out to farmers for cultivation, and the annual rent was paid in the form of "negotiated rent", that is, all proceeds of land were divided between the farmers and the company on a 40% and 60% basis. By adopting this tenancy system, Tonghai Reclamation Company was able to take the whole situation into account and plan accordingly to perform the tasks such as farmland water conservancy and agricultural technology promotion that cannot be done by a single farmer family alone.

沿海垦殖开发

1901年，通海垦牧公司创办后，张謇等人经过10年的努力，到1910年时可利用的土地增多，加上大生各厂对棉花的需求量扩大，开始获益。因此，张謇等从1913年开始，再次掀起一个兴办盐垦公司的热潮。到1920年为止，先后成立了大有晋、大豫等10多家公司。于是，江苏东部南起启东吕四场、北至阜宁的陈家港，在绵延600多公里的冲击平原上，相继出现了大小盐垦公司70余家，土地面积约450万亩，已垦土地面积也超过70万亩。大片荒地的开发，为大批通、崇、海、启移民开辟了新的生活途径。至20世纪30年代，淮南盐垦各公司总管理处所属的17个公司，共建了25个市镇、474间仓库、1761.2公里公路，架设了631公里电话线，建立95所合作社、56所中小学、10所诊疗所。垦区的经济社会发展取得显著成果。

Development of Coastal Reclamation

Through ten years of sound management, available land and Dasheng's demand for cotton began to increase. Therefore, in 1910, Tonghai Reclamation Company reaped initial benefits. In 1913, Zhang Jian started another round of setting up reclamation companies. More than ten companies had been established up to 1920. As a result, there were in total more than 70 reclamation companies of various sizes in the plain of the eastern part of Jiangsu, which stretched for more than 600 kilometers from Lüsi field of Qidong in the south to Chenjia Port of Funing in the north. These reclamation companies covered about 300,000-hectare land, among which more than 46,666 hectares had been reclaimed. The development of large areas of wasteland opened up a new way of life for a large number of immigrants from Nantong. By the 1930s, the 17 companies under the Administration of Huainan Reclamation had built 25 towns, 474 warehouses, 1,761.2 kilometers of roads, 631 kilometers of telephone lines, 95 cooperatives, 56 primary and secondary schools, and 10 dispensaries. The economic and social development of the reclamation area achieved remarkable results.

植树造林

1901年，张謇在《变法平议》中谈到农业改革时提到：凡各府州县辖境，三年内责成农商官，毋许有不林之山，不谷不牧之地……。在兴办实业的同时，张謇十分重视植树造林，多次强调植树造林对平衡生态的重要意义。在担任北洋政府农商总长期间，张謇主持拟定了中国最早的一部《森林法》，此外还拟定了《森林法实施细则》等一系列法律条文和规章制度，推动植树造林。针对黄河、长江、珠江等流域的水患，他主张设保安林的编栽局，负责植树造林事宜。张謇支持在金陵大学农科内开设一所林业学校（即今南京农业大学的前身）。在南通，张謇在五山地区植树建设苗圃、植物园，主张城市道路“植树木以表之”，还发动人们在捍海堤两侧广植树木，以抗击沿海风潮，对新开垦的农田起到了保护作用。

Afforestation

In 1901, Zhang Jian mentioned in the *Commentary on Reform Movement* that the agricultural officials should see to it that in three years, there should be no land left unused and no mountains uncovered with woods. Zhang Jian attached great importance to afforestation and emphasized many times the important role of afforestation in ecological balance. During his tenure as the Minister of Agriculture and Commerce in Beiyang Government, Zhang Jian presided over the drafting of the earliest *Law on Forest* in China, and also drafted a series of legal provisions and regulations such as the *Rules for the Implementation of the Forest Law* to promote afforestation and improve the living environment. In view of the recurrent floods in the Yellow River, Yangtze River and Pearl River basins, he suggested setting up a specialized bureau to take charge of afforestation. Zhang Jian supported the establishment of a forestry school in the agricultural department of Jinling University (the predecessor of Nanjing Agricultural University). He proposed lining the streets with trees to purify the air and decorate the city. On top of that, he mobilized people to plant trees on both sides of the sea dikes which helped to protect the newly reclaimed farmland.

新的城市形象

1914年，在南通老城东、西、南大街交汇处的旧州县衙的谯楼前，一座钟楼拔地而起。钟楼由通州师范学校毕业生孙支夏设计，高6层，为当时南通城最高的建筑。"畴昔是州今是县"，张謇通过这一建筑符号宣告着南通城旧历史的终结和一个崭新时代的到来。

近代南通城市空间变化最显著的地方，除了钟楼，就是城南濠河两岸至桃坞路一线新的城市中心，城南别业、上海银行、濠南别业、淮海实业银行、通明电器公司、有斐馆、商会大厦、更俗剧场、南通俱乐部等一大批高大的西式建筑相继出现。在满足一个城市近代化发展的功能需求时，张謇用建筑这种最直观的物体作为城市展品展示给市民和来访者，在中西建筑风格的交融中传播着现代的理念和开放的精神。

Transforming the Urban Image

In 1914, a clock tower was erected in front of the watchtower of the former County Office in the center of Nantong city. Designed by Sun Zhixia, a graduate of Tongzhou Normal School, the clock tower was six-story high, the tallest building in Nantong City at that time. By this architectural symbol, Zhang Jian announced the end of the old Nantong and the coming of the new era.

The most remarkable change of urban space in modern Nantong, besides the clock tower, is the new city center along the banks of Hao River to Taowu Road in the south of the city. There emerged a large number of tall western-style buildings represented by Chengnan Villa, Shanghai Bank, Haonan Villa, Huaihai Industrial Bank, Tongming Electric Company, Youfei Hotel, Chamber of Commerce Building, Gengsu Theatre and Nantong Club. While meeting the functional needs of a city's modernization, architecture as the most intuitive object was displayed to citizens and visitors, spreading modernity and openness through the interplay of Chinese and Western architectural styles.

强健身心

南通是著名的体育之乡，这与张謇早期推动也不无关系。1917年，张謇与张詧捐资在城南兴建了南通最早的体育场——第一公共体育场。体育场占地20余亩，设有足球场、篮球场、排球场等，让市民前来运动锻炼，且不收任何费用。1923年，张謇又主持修建了南通第二公共体育场，面积将近第一公共体育场的两倍。一座县城同时拥有两个体育场，这在当时是极为罕见的。在唐闸，1913年，张謇、张詧兄弟开始筹建唐闸公园，次年建成，成为工人休息的重要场所。此后，张謇还借鉴唐闸公园的建设经验，于1917年在濠河西南隅修建了五公园，同时向公众免费开放。张謇亲自谱写《南通公园歌》："南通胜哉江淮皋，公园秩秩城之濠。自北自东自西自南中央包。北河有球场枪垛可以豪。东河有女子小儿可以嬉且遨。南可棋饮西可池泳舟可漕。"由此可见张謇致力民众身心健康的良苦用心。

Strengthening the Body and Mind

Nantong is a renowned cradle for sports champions and some of the credit goes to the efforts made by Zhang Jian. In 1917, Zhang Jian and his elder brother Zhang Cha donated money to build the first stadium in the south of Nantong, which was also the first public stadium in China. In 1923, Zhang Jian presided over the construction of the second public stadium in Nantong, which was nearly twice the size of the first one. It was extremely rare at that time for a county to have two stadiums. In 1913, Zhang Jian and Zhang Cha started to build Tangzha Park, which was completed the following year and became an important resting place for workers. After that, Zhang Jian built the Five Parks in the southwest corner of Haohe River in 1917, which were open to the public for free. Zhang Jian composed the "Song of Nantong Parks" in person, which goes like "Nantong is a wonderful place to live in with so many parks and the glistening Haohe River. Five parks are scattered in the five directions of downtown. In the northern part of Haohe River, there are courts for playing balls. In the eastern part of Haohe River, there are places for children to play games. In the northern part, people can play chess and have a drink. In the western part, people can swim in the river and row boats." This shows Zhang Jian's devotion to the physical and mental health of the people.

沪通之间，折苇可渡

南通与上海虽然只有一江之隔，但在近代，因长江天险阻隔，交通并不便利。1879年4月24日，张謇从海门青龙港启程去上海，结果在路上颠簸了四天才到达。当时的上海，是“万国竞争之场、商战之冲”，沪通之间的交通如此困难，这让张謇暗下决心改善交通状况。

鉴于上海对大生企业发展的重要地位，1899年7月，张謇积极争取南洋大臣刘坤一同意大生纱厂租轮船往来通沪之间运送物资，初步解决了大生纱厂早期的货物运输问题。1900年，为运输大生物料设立大生轮船公司；1903年，创办了经营内河航运的大达小轮公司；1904年，在天生港成立了经营码头业务和长江航运的大达轮步公司；1905年，在外商林立的外滩成立了上海大达轮步公司，并担任经理，在上海十六铺建造了大达码头。经过张謇的努力，沪通之间的交通得到实质性的改进，上海的物资、人才、资金等能够及时快捷抵达南通，为南通的发展注入了活力。“沪通之间，折苇可渡”，早年文人的浪漫，此时已逐渐成为现实。

Sailing between Shanghai and Nantong on a Piece of Reed

Nantong was separated with Shanghai by only a strip of Yangtze River, but in modern China, the Yangtze River as natural barrier made transportation inconvenient. On April 24, 1879, Zhang Jian set off from Qinglong Port in Haimen, and it took him four days to reach Shanghai. At that time, Shanghai was "the strategic point for business competition", and the traffic between Shanghai and Nantong was so difficult that Zhang Jian made his mind to improve the traffic.

In view of the importance of Shanghai to the development of Dasheng Cotton Mill, in July 1899, Zhang Jian won over the support of Liu Kunyi, minister in charge of coastal affairs in East China. The minister permitted Dasheng to rent ships to transport materials between Nantong and Shanghai. In 1900, Zhang Jian set up Dasheng Shipping Company for the transportation of Dasheng materials. In 1903, he established Dada Ferry Company specializing inland navigation. In 1904, he set up Dada Steamship Company in Tiansheng Port, which operated wharf business and shipping on Yangtze River. In 1905, he set up Shanghai Dada Steamship Company in the Bund of Shanghai where stood a number of foreign companies, and acted as the manager. He also built Dada Wharf in Shiliupu Port. Through Zhang Jian's efforts, the traffic between Shanghai and Nantong was substantially improved, and the materials, talents and capital from Shanghai could reach Nantong in time, which injected vitality into the development of Nantong. The romantic imagination that "Between Nantong and Shanghai I can sail, on a piece of reed" had gradually turned to a reality.

至诚至信

惜才重德

Treating People with Sincerity and Valuing Talents

敬篤信忠

忠信笃敬

1918年，张謇在尊孔会第一次演说中强调，“欲昌明孔学，宜就子臣弟友、忠信笃敬八字做起。子为孝亲，臣为卫国，弟为敬长，友为爱人，此属于分际也；忠则不贰，信则不欺，笃则不忘，敬则不偷，此属于行为也。人能明分际而谨行为，斯尽人道矣”。

“诚”与“信”，是中国传统文化的重要内涵，是传统社会人人必须遵守的基本道德规范。自幼接受儒家传统教育的张謇，一生以诚信作为自己的行为准则，并以此教育其子张孝若和通海学子。张謇也曾说过这样一些话：“生平待人坦怀相与，不事机诈”，“诚者天之道”，“修身之道，固多端也，即就不说谎不骗人做去亦可矣”……张謇不仅将诚信视作个人的道德范畴，还将其与现代企业的信用联系起来。在数十年的实业生涯中，张謇一直恪守这四个字，让大生企业集团始终保持着良好的信誉。

Loyalty, Faithfulness, Assurance, and Respect

In 1918, Zhang Jian stressed in his first address in the Society for Venerating Confucianism that "To advocate Confucianism, we should start from its basic teachings. Namely, children should be filial to their parents, subjects should safeguard the country, the younger should respect the elderly, and people should live in amity with each other. That shows sense of propriety. Besides, loyalty, faithfulness, assurance and respect are code of behaviors. If one acts with sense of propriety and be discreet in their behaviors, he or she can be called a decent person."

"Honesty" and "credibility" are important elements of traditional Chinese culture and the basic moral codes in traditional society. Zhang Jian, who received traditional Confucian education since his childhood, made honesty and credibility his code of conduct throughout his life, and taught his son Zhang Xiaoruo and the students of Nantong with it. Zhang Jian also said, "I treat people frankly, and I don't cheat", "Honesty is heavenly law", "The ways to cultivate moral character are varied, and not lying or cheating is among them." He not only regarded honesty and credibility as personal moral code, but also linked it with the modern enterprises. Throughout his decades of developing industry, Zhang Jian has adhered to the Confucian moral code, so that Dasheng Group has always maintained a good reputation.

坚苦自立，忠实不欺

清光绪二十九年（1903）四月初一日，通州师范学校正式开校。张謇亲临学校发表了演讲。他勉励广大师生说：“孟子曰：‘人皆可以为尧舜。’愿诸君开拓胸襟，立定志愿，求人之长，成己之用；不妄自菲薄，自然不妄自尊大。忠实不欺，坚苦自立，成我通州之学风。”此后他又亲笔书写了“坚苦自立，忠实不欺”二语作为校训，制成扁额悬挂在师范学校礼堂。他说此二语是自己平生自励自勉的座右铭，现在用来勖勉广大师生，以此塑造南通全新的校风学风和城市精神。

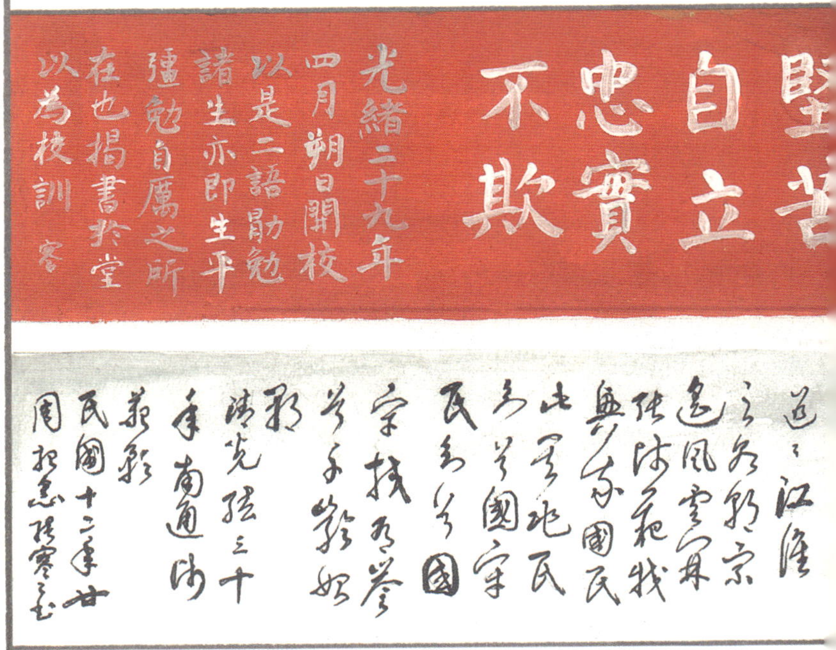

Self-reliance and Faithfulness

On the first day of April in 1903, Tongzhou Normal School was officially opened. Zhang Jian delivered a speech, in which he encouraged the teachers and students that "As Mencius said, all men can be Yao Shun (two legendary sage kings). May all of you open your mind and set your mind on learning from others and then practicing what you learned on yourself. You may neither be conceited nor belittle yourself. You should be faithful rather than deceitful, be hardworking and self-reliant to form good atmosphere in Tongzhou." After that, he wrote "Self-Reliance and Faithfulness" as the school motto, which was then inscribed on the horizontal board hung in the auditorium of the school. He said that the two words were the motto of his own for self-motivation, and now he used them to inspire teachers and students, so as to shape the new school spirit and city spirit of Nantong.

廠約
1
2
3
4

以公容错

张謇对所任用的人、对于办事得力的人，会积极争取较为丰厚的奖励，以资鼓励。对于犯有过失的员工，张謇也是区别对待，在拟定的《厂约》中有“公过”和“私过”之分。所谓“公过”，就是指主观无错，好心办了坏事等；所谓“私过”，即指营私舞弊，亏空犯规，以及偷懒误事等主观上的过错。张謇对犯“公过”的人，只要不说谎，一般以宽容为主，希望其从经验教训中有所长进；而对于犯“私过”的人，一旦发现毫不留情，绝不宽容，轻辄罚薪，重则开除，以免妨碍全局。作为一名儒商，张謇主张“以诚待人、以信接物、以义取利”，在他的人格魅力影响下，大生企业员工的凝聚力进一步增强。

Tolerating Unintentional Mistakes and Upholding Fairness

Zhang Jian provided generous rewards as encouragement for the people he appointed and for those who did a good job. For employees who committed faults, Zhang Jian treated them differently. In the *Factory Convention*, faults were classified as "unintsentional faults" and "intentional faults". By "unintentional", it referred to the situation that good intentions brought about bad results; by "intentional", it meant abusing one's position for personal gains, embezzlement or misconduct caused by laziness. For those who committed "unintentional faults", as long as they did not lie, Zhang Jian would generally be tolerant, hoping that they would learn from the lessons; while for those who committed "intentional faults", he would not show any mercy or tolerance. As a scholar-merchant, Zhang Jian advocated "treating people with sincerity, handling things with integrity, and taking benefits without resorting to dirty tricks". Under the influence of his charisma, the employees of Dasheng bonded together in a closer union.

跨国的忘年交

特来克（1890—1919），荷兰水利工程师。早年就读于荷兰工程专科学校，毕业后因擅长河海水利工程而继承父业（其父奈格是荷兰著名的水利工程师）。1916年，特来克受张謇之聘，到南通任保坍会工程师，负责保坍筑楗工程。在南通工作期间，特来克积极参与现场勘查，不仅督造沿江水楗，还为南通、如皋、海门等地水利事业日夜操心，得到张謇、张詧兄弟和社会各界人士的好评。1916年，受聘仅两个月的特来克就完成了《南通保坍计划报告书》。1918年，特来克设计督造的遥望港九门闸开工。1919年夏，正在工地视察的特来克不幸染病去世，终年29岁。张謇一方面为特来克举行公葬，并将其安葬在剑山南麓，亲自撰写墓表，镌石以表纪念；一方面争取徐世昌代表国家为特来克颁发褒词，以肯定外籍专家对中国所做的贡献。

Transnational Friendship

De Rijke (1890-1919) was a Dutch hydraulic engineer. After graduation from Dutch Academy of Engineering, he followed his father's steps as he was good at river and sea water engineering (his father Nigel is a famous water engineer in Holland). In 1916, he was hired by Zhang Jian to work as an engineer in Nantong, in charge of the dike reinforcement project. During his stay in Nantong, De Rijke participated in the site survey, supervised the construction of dike reinforcement, and worked day and night for the water conservancy projects in Nantong, Rugao, Haimen and other places. He was highly praised by Zhang Jian, Zhang Cha and people from all walks of life. Within two months after his appointment in 1916, De Rijke had finished *Report on the Dike Reinforcement Plan of Nantong*. In 1918, the Jiumen sluice gate of Yaowang Port designed and supervised by De Rijke went into operation. In the summer of 1919, De Rijke unfortunately contracted disease when inspecting the construction site, and passed away at the age of 29. Not only did Zhang Jian write for and engrave the tombstone to commemorate him, he also persuaded Xu Shichang (the then president of the Republic of China) to issue a commendation for De Rijke on behalf of the state to recognize the foreign expert's contribution to China.

器重才俊

张謇对杰出能干的有志青年十分器重。

宋希尚（1896—1982），浙江嵊县人。民国六年（1917），宋希尚毕业于南京河海工程专门学校，由校方选送至南通保坍会实习，并成为荷兰水利工程师特来克的助手。特来克去世后，宋希尚临危受命，负责办理遥望港工程，经过一年的时间，将其完工，得到张謇的赞赏。当得知宋希尚有赴美深造、考察欧美水利，为今后从事水利事业做准备的远大抱负时，张謇表示一定会促成此事。两年后，宋希尚参与的青龙港船闸工程顺利完工，张謇便践行自己的诺言，资助宋希尚留学美国。出国前，宋希尚特地来到濠阳小筑向张謇辞别，张謇“整襟肃容，自房内步送，……复命大开正门而至门口，乃停步拱手面嘱”，宋希尚离开后，张謇立于门口目送，“直至淮海银行转角不见为止”。

Valuing Talented People

Zhang Jian held great respect for outstanding and capable young people.

Song Xishang (1896–1982) was a native of Sheng County, Zhejiang Province. In 1917, Song graduated from Nanjing Hohai Engineering Specialized School and was recommended by the school as an intern for the Nantong Association for Dike Reinforcement. He acted as assistant of the Dutch water conservancy engineer, De Rijke. After the death of De Rijke, Song Xishang was entrusted with the project of Yaowang Port and finished it after one year, which was appreciated by Zhang Jian. When he learned that Song Xishang had the aspiration to go to the United States for further study and to learn about European and American water conservancy, Zhang Jian said he would definitely help to bring it about. Two years later, upon the successful completion of the Qinglong Port Lock project, Zhang Jian fulfilled his promise and sponsored Song Xishang to study in the United States. Before leaving the country, Song Xishang visited Hao Yang Villa to bid farewell to Zhang Jian, who "straightened up and sent him away from the room.... ordered to open the main door, and then stopped to bid him farewell with a cupped-hand salute". "After Song Xishang's departure, Zhang Jian stood at the door and watched him leave until he disappeared around the corner."

須知無子弟不可為家
無人才不可爲國

涵养家风

1921年，69岁的张謇辑取诸葛亮、朱熹等7位古人的教子格言刻于石碑上，内容涉及立志修身等方面，张謇用这一《家训》来告诫子孙。此碑现存于南通博物苑内。

张謇一直注重家风家教，46岁得子怡祖（孝若），因此始终把张孝若的教育作为重要的事情来对待。张謇让儿子接受中西方的教育内容，还专门为儿子请了外籍教师。因张孝若长年不在父亲身边，张謇先后给他写了许多家信，约100余封。

1915年2月2日，在北洋政府担任农商总长的张謇给张孝若写信，信中写道“须知无子弟不可为家，无人才不可为国，努力求学，厚养志气，以待为国雪耻。”此时的张謇在北京见袁世凯急于复辟帝制，与日本帝国主义进行着政治交易，有感而发，借此勉励、督促儿子成才。在张謇的家庭教育下，张孝若留学美国，获得学士学位后归国，在继承张謇事业中表现出杰出的才干。

Nurturing Family Spirit

In 1921, at the age of 69, Zhang Jian carved the motto of seven ancient scholars about cultivating moral character, including those of Zhuge Liang and Zhu Xi, on a stone tablet. He used this family motto to caution his children and grandchildren. This stone tablet is now kept in Nantong Museum.

Zhang Jian made his son Zhang Xiaoruo receive both Chinese and Western education, and hired a foreign teacher for him. As Zhang Xiaoruo was away from his father for years on end, Zhang Jian wrote about 100 letters to him.

On February 2, 1915, Zhang Jian, then Minister of Agriculture and Commerce in the Beiyang Government, wrote a letter to Zhang Xiaoruo. The letter went “Without younger generation, a family cannot be called family; without talents, a country cannot compete on the world arena. You shall study hard and lift your spirits, so that you can avenge the shame of your country.” At that time, seeing that Yuan Shikai was eager to restore the imperial system and making political deals with the Japanese imperialists, Zhang Jian was distressed and could not help urging his son to become a man of talent. Under Zhang Jian’s family education, Zhang Xiaoruo went to study in the United States and returned home with a bachelor’s degree, showing outstanding talent in following Zhang Jian’s steps.

德生

大一

地马

天牛

Cultivating Moral Integrity and Being Diligent all Through Life

天地之大德曰生

生生不息

张謇创办大生纱厂以“为通州民生计，亦即为中国利源计”为目的，厂名“大生”取自《周易·系辞》中“天地之大德曰生”一句，以此表达其办厂初衷。张謇以后兴办的许多企业仍多以“生”命名，如资生铁冶厂、广生油厂、泽生水利公司、阜生丝厂、颐生酒厂、懋生房产公司等等，无不体现“民生”的重要。张謇曾对好友说：“天地之大德曰生。这句话的解释，就是说一切政治及学问，最低的期望要使大多数的老百姓，都能得到最低水平线上的生活……换句话说，没有饭吃的人，要他有饭吃；生活困苦的，使他能够逐渐提高。这就是号称儒者应尽的本分。”这道出了张謇一生全部事业的出发点和最终归宿。

The Greatest Virtue Is People's Well-being

The factory name "Dasheng" was chosen from the phrase "The greatest virtue on earth is people's well-being" in *Book of Changes*, which expressed the original intention of the factory to improve people's well-being. Many enterprises established by Zhang Jian afterwards were still named after "Sheng", such as Zisheng Iron and Steel Factory, Guangsheng Oil Factory, Zesheng Water Conservancy Company, Fusheng Silk Factory, Yisheng Winery, and Maosheng Real Estate Company, which all reflected the importance of "people's livelihood". Zhang Jian once said to his friend, "The greatest virtue on earth is people's well-being. It means that the minimum expectation of all politics and learning is to enable most people to live above subsistence level. In other words, those who starve can have food to eat; those who are badly off can improve their life gradually. This is the duty of the so-called Confucianist." This is the starting point and ultimate destination of Zhang Jian's undertakings in his whole life.

人道之存，人格之成

张謇把“地方自治”概括为实业、教育、慈善三个方面。他这样阐述三者的关系：“窃謇以国家之强，本于自治，自治之本，在实业教育，而弥缝其不及者，惟赖慈善。”对于慈善事业，张謇付出过很多的心血。

张謇还把教育和慈善两大事业作过比较，他说：“查地方自治，以进增社会之能率，弥补人民之缺憾为其职志。而进行之事业，属于积极之充实者，最要为教育，属于消极之救济者，最要为慈善。教育发展，则能率于增进，慈善周遍，憾于以弥补。”慈善、公益是进行“地方自治”的重要组成。“慈善”的目的也是“进增社会之能率，弥补人民之缺憾”，这是区别于传统的“善举”“义行”等施舍、赈济活动的，具有明确的救亡图存、改良社会的近代观念。

Charity Shows Human Sympathy and Cultivates Moral Integrity

Zhang Jian summarized “self-governance at local level” into three aspects: industry, education and charity, and he elaborated the relationship among them in this way: “I personally believe that the strength of a country comes from self-governance, and the essence of self-governance lies in industry and education. The only thing that can make up for its shortcomings is charity.” Zhang Jian devoted much effort to charity.

Zhang Jian also made a comparison between the two major undertakings of education and charity. He put it that “self-governance serves the purposes of improving social efficiency and making for the imperfections for the people”. While education is more proactive, charity is relatively reactive. Education and charity are important components of “self-governance at local level”. The purpose of charity is to make up for the imperfections of the people, which is different from the traditional “good deeds” of alms-giving and relief activities, and has a clear modern concept of saving and improving society.

愛

关注孤幼伤残

张謇一生兴办了一大批的社会救助、优待和抚恤的慈善机构，门类齐全，涉及面广，对因年老、失怙、伤残、失业、疾病等无助人群实施了较大范围的救助。其中关注残疾儿童、使之受教育并发挥作用的理念尤其值得钦佩。

1913年，张謇开始筹措资金，在狼山北麓购地六亩许兴建狼山盲哑学校。1916年11月学校开学，设盲、哑两科，以“培养盲哑师资，造就盲哑使其有独立自存之能力”为宗旨，张謇亲自担任了盲哑学校的首任校长。盲哑学校培养了许多有技能的劳动者，毕业生中有受聘到商务印书馆等书局任职的。在1929年西湖博览会上，学校提供的58件参展展品大受中外人士称道。

Caring for Orphans, Children and the Disabled

During his lifetime, Zhang Jian set up a large number of charitable institutions for social assistance, preferential treatment and compassionate care, providing a wide range of assistance and care to helpless people suffering from old age, disability, unemployment or illness. His idea of caring for disabled children and educating them is particularly admirable.

In 1913, Zhang Jian started to raise funds to build Wolf Mountain School for the Blind and Mute at the northern foot of Wolf Mountain. The school was launched in November 1916 with two subjects regarding the blind and mute, and Zhang Jian assumed office of the president. Aiming at training teachers for the blind and mute and teaching the blind and mute to live independently, the school trained many skilled workers, and some of the graduates were employed in bookstores such as the Commercial Press. At the 1929 West Lake Exposition, the 58 exhibits provided by the school were highly praised by Chinese and foreign visitors.

张謇卖字

状元张謇的书法为世所推崇。从创办大生纱厂开始，张謇即以卖字补贴旅费，从未在纱厂经费中支用一分。

1906年，张謇在唐闸建新育婴堂，经费不足，即公开登报卖字募集经费。此后，随着各项公益慈善事业的费用所需不断增加，张謇在百忙中不忘以字易资。他经常在上海、南通各大报纸上发布鬻字启示，在这些启事中张謇说，不论何人，只要出钱，皆可以像役使牛马一样役使我，帮助我献爱于疾苦无助之人，效力于地方自治。1922年，大生企业集团发生了前所未有的危机，各项慈善公益事业的经费更为困难。年逾古稀的张謇为南通的各项事业殚精竭虑、苦苦支撑。这时报纸上又出现了张謇的《为慈善公益鬻字启》，这次卖字定期为一月，而事实上竟持续了两年多的时间。

Selling Calligraphy Works

The calligraphy of Scholar Zhang Jian is highly regarded by the public. Starting from the founding of Dasheng Cotton Mill, Zhang Jian often sold calligraphy to cover his travel expenses, and he never spent a single cent of the expenses of the factory.

In 1906, Zhang Jian built a new nursery school in Tangzha, but the fund was not enough, so he published a notice in the newspaper to raise funds. Since then, as the expenses for various charitable causes increased, Zhang Jian often sold off his calligraphy for raising fund despite tight schedule. His announcements for selling calligraphy appeared frequently on the newspapers of Nantong and Shanghai, which said that "I am grateful for anyone who buys my calligraphy. In doing so, they assisted me in helping the disadvantaged and contributing to self-governance." In 1922, the Dasheng Group was in an unprecedented crisis, and it was even more difficult to finance the charitable causes. Zhang Jian, who was in his 70s, tried his best to support Nantong's various undertakings. His *Letter of Sale for Charity* appeared again in the newspaper. This time, the sale originally intended for one month lasted for more than two years.

析產書
要之此
後之皮
骨心血
當為盡
畀犧牲
不能復
為子孫
牛馬則
余二人志
願之所
同也

皮骨心血，当为世界牺牲

1904年，张謇和他哥哥张詧分家，他们写了一份“析产书”，在文末，他们以这样的言辞表明二人共同的志愿：“要之，此后之皮骨心血，当为世界牺牲，不能复为子孙牛马，则余二人志愿之所同也。”“为世牛马”“为世界牺牲”，这是张謇经常用于表达人生观的朴实表述，也是他躬行实践的人生宗旨。正是有这样的人生追求和精神动力，张謇成就了常人所难以匹及的事业。

My Mortal Body Should Be Sacrificed for the Public

In 1904, Zhang Jian and his brother, Zhang Cha, divided family property and lived apart. For this cause, they wrote the *Letter of Dividing Property* and at the end of the letter, they expressed their common will in these words “we will sacrifice our mortal body for the public, and we will not be able to attend to our children”. “To serve like beasts of burden for the public” and “to sacrifice for the public” are the unadorned phrases that Zhang Jian often used to express his outlook on life, and they are also the purpose of his life. It is with this pursuit of life and spiritual motivation that Zhang Jian achieved a career that is beyond the reach of ordinary people.

叫我做公僕可以做衆僕不行
張謇語
大生紗廠第八屆說略

“公仆”和“众仆”

当大生纱厂盈利稳增时，张謇开始动用大生纱厂的资金进行集团化扩张，并开始兴办教育、文化、公益事业。有股东感到张謇的做法触犯了他们的利益，股东大会上有人对大生过多的业外投资提出反对意见，张謇严词回应说：我一直和大家说，叫我做“公仆”可以，做“众仆”不行！

在张謇看来，“众仆”只是为“有限股东”服务的“牛马”。他拥有更远大的抱负和更坚强的信念，那就是为救亡图存、民族振兴。“须有国权，乃能有商利者，公仆之义也”，所做“公仆”就是要超越某个企业、有限股东的狭小利益，是为国家、为社会、为大众谋利益的“公仆”，用他的话说，即“借各股东资本之力，以成鄙人建设一新世界雏型之志，以雪中国地方不能自治之耻，虽牛马于社会而不辞也”。

“Public Servant” and “Servant for the Majority”

As the profit of Dasheng Cotton Mill increased steadily, Zhang Jian used the capital of Dasheng for group expansion and started to develop education, culture and public welfare undertakings. Some shareholders felt that Zhang Jian’s practice damaged their interests, and at the shareholders’ meeting, some people raised objections to the excessive investment outside of industries, to which Zhang Jian responded sternly, “I have told all people repeatedly that I can be a ‘public servant’ but not a ‘servant for the majority’!”

In Zhang Jian’s view, “servant for the majority” is beast of burden serving “limited shareholders” only. He had more ambitions and stronger beliefs, that is to save the country and revitalize the nation. “To be a public servant means to transcend the narrow interests of a certain enterprise and shareholders. Public servants should serve the interest of the country, the society and the public.” “I would like to pool the strength of stakeholders to fulfil the ambition of building a self-governed society and avenge the insult that Chinese are not capable of self-governance. For that purpose, I would not shrink from serving the public like.”

儉可以凝貞苦之心可以養高尚之節可以立實業之本可以廣教育之施
張謇在通州師範學校開學訓話時語

凝贞苦之心，养高尚之节

1907年3月10日，通州师范学校开学，张謇到学校训话，一开头他就给学生们提出几个问题："世何以须教育？教育何以须师范？师范之养成，以何为重？师范之希望，以何为先？"张謇举出了孔子、孟子的言论，向同学们指出，师范教育要以俭为重、以俭为先。

张謇把"俭"作为他对年轻人的鞭策和要求，是其人生经验使然。张謇出生于寒门，从小就养成了勤勉节俭任劳耐苦的习惯。所以他和同学们分享的是他成功的经验：俭不仅可以使人养成坚贞耐苦的意志、高尚美好的节操，还可以通过节俭，让实业、教育建设得到更多的投入。

Tenacity and Lofty Ideas

On March 10, 1907, Zhang Jian attended the opening ceremony of Tongzhou Normal School and addressed the students. At the beginning, he asked the students several questions, "Why does the world need education? Why is teacher training necessary for education? What is the priority for training teachers? What is the thing we expect most of normal school?" Citing the words of Confucius and Mencius, Zhang Jian pointed out that frugality should be the priority of teacher training.

The fact that Zhang Jian took "frugality" as a spur and requirement for his young people was the result of his life experience. Born into a humble family, Zhang Jian developed the habit of diligence, frugality and hard work from his childhood. Therefore, he shared his successful experience with the students: frugality helps people to develop a strong will and a noble mind to endure hardships, and the money saved allows more investment into industry and education.

牛车简从

张謇是一介寒儒出身，深知民间疾苦，成为乡绅之后亦未忘本。他在通海一带勘察荒地水情时，不准鸣锣开道，不坐轿子，而是坐农民的牛车，一心想着为老百姓办实事。其子张孝若曾回忆，“(父亲) 晚年巡视河工，海滩上只有笨重土制的牛车，还是敞篷，坐上去十分不舒服，我父处之泰然，每天走百十里路”。

Travelling on Oxcart

Zhang Jian was a humble scholar. He knew well the sufferings of ordinary people and did not forget his roots even after he became a country squire. When he surveyed the water conditions of the wasteland around Tonghai, he didn't allow entourage to beat gongs to clear the way or take a sedan chair (for officials in feudal times). Instead, he took a farmer's oxcart, thinking of doing practical things for the people. His son Zhang Xiaoruo recalled that "Father in his late years only took bulky open-top oxcart. It was quite uncomfortable to ride on the oxcart, but my father remained unruffled and travelled about hundreds of miles on it a day."

刻意節儉為自立之圖非常之備

刻意节俭

张孝若在回忆其父日常生活时写道：“他穿的衣衫，有几件差不多穿了三四年之久，平常穿的大概都有十年八年。如果袜子破了，总是加补丁，要补到无可再补，方才换一件新品。每天饭菜，不过一荤一素一汤，没有特客，向来不杀鸡鸭。写信用的信封，都是拿人家来信翻了过来，再将平日人家寄来的红纸请帖裁了下来，加贴一条在中间，日常都用这翻过来的信封，有时候包药的纸，或者废纸，拿过来起稿子或者写便条用。……平常走路，看见一个钉，一块板，都捡起来聚在一起，等到相当的时候去应用它。” 张謇居家生活如此精细节约，与他的收入水平和社会地位如此不相称，实在让人难以想象。张謇的节俭有更深层的思考，他曾和张孝若说：“刻意节俭，为自立之图、非常之备。”张謇在节俭的言传身教中体现着一种自立精神和忧患意识。

Intended Frugality

Zhang Xiaoruo wrote of his father's daily life, “He has worn some clothes for three or four years, and usually kept his clothes for a long time, like eight to ten years. He always adds patches to worn socks until they are beyond mending, and only then, he changes a new pair. The daily meal includes but a course of meat, a vegetable dish and a bowl of soup. Chicken and duck will not be served on table when there are no special guests. He often reuses the letter envelop sent to him. He sometimes uses the paper package, or waste paper for writing a manuscript or a note. When walking on streets, he picks deserted nails and cardboards, and collects them for future use.” It is unimaginable that Zhang Jian lived such frugal life, which was so disproportionate to his income and social status. Zhang Jian has deep reflection on frugality, and he once talked with Zhang Xiaoruo, “Intended frugality is for self-reliance and emergency.” Zhang Jian embodied a spirit of self-reliance and a sense of worry for unexpected in his teachings and practice of frugality.

捐

聚财和散财

张謇生活简朴，却经常“公私不分”，将私人收入充作各种公益用途。他说：“应该用的，为人用的，一千一万都得不眨眼顺手就用；自用的，消耗的，连一个钱都得想想，都得节省。”又说：“有钱人的势焰，实在难受，所以我非有钱不可。但是那班有了钱的人是一毛不拔做守财奴，我可是抱定有了钱，非全用掉不可。”还说：“人单单寻钱聚财不算本事，要会用钱散财。”

南通的社会事业一直面临着经费不足的问题，张謇将个人的金钱收入大量资助到文教慈善公益事业中去，总体出资情况难有确切的统计。张謇在去世前一年谈到他对教育、慈善等事业的资助时说：“用于地方及他处教育、慈善、公益可记者一百五十余万外，合叔兄所用已二百余万，謇单独负债又八九十万余元。”显然，资助的金额是非常大的。

Gathering and Giving Away Wealth

It is Zhang Jian's habit to lead a simple and frugal life. However, Zhang Jian often made no distinction between public and private interests, and used his private income for various public welfare purposes. He used to say, "I wouldn't have even little hesitation to spend money on what should be done for the public, but I begrudge even a single penny spent for personal use and consumption." Zhang Jian said, "The bigwigs are usually swollen with arrogance. I could hardly bear with it, so I must earn more fortune. But compared with the misters who are unwilling to give up even a hair, I am determined to spend all the money I have on public interests."

Insufficient funding had always been a problem for social undertakings in Nantong. Zhang Jian contributed a lot of his personal income to the undertakings of education, charity and public welfare, and it was difficult to have exact statistics on the overall funding. A year before his death, Zhang Jian said , "My recorded spending on education, charity and public welfare in Nantong and other places is more than one and a half million yuan. The overall spending totaled to more than two million yuan if the money contributed by my uncles and brothers is added. Other than that, the debt borne by myself alone amounts to more than eight hundred thousand yuan."

下走之為世牛馬終歲無停趾私以為今日之人當以勞死不當以逸生下走尚未忍言勞也……
張謇此信
留住了三位請辭的老師繼續留任後為南通教育做出了很大的貢獻

为世牛马，终岁无停趾

1909年的一天，通州师范学校的缪文功、李元蘅、顾公毅三位老师提出辞职。这三位老师是南通教育界的重要骨干，他们的辞职让张謇深感不安，他随即提笔给他们写信：各位老师相率请辞，是因为学问不足于用，还是因为教学太辛苦？学问提高是理论和阅历的结合形成，一面研究，一面实践，正是追求学问提升弥补不足的方法，这可不是辞职的理由；如果是因为太辛苦的话，那就看看我是怎么想的，怎么做的。张謇说：我就像世间辛勤耕耘奔走的牛马，终年都没有停歇的时候，我认为今日之人，应当辛苦劳作而死，而不应该安逸闲适而生。我整天奔忙也从不愿意说自己辛苦啊！现在正是民族危亡的时刻，惟有教育才能救国救民，希望诸位贤士相互勉励，协助我一起为南通的教育事业发展而努力吧！三位老师为张謇的精神所打动，继续在南通的教育界任职，后来都做出了积极的贡献。

Serving the People all Through Life

One day in 1909, three teachers from Tongzhou Normal School, namely Miao Wenkong, Li Yuanheng and Gu Gongyi, resigned. Their resignation deeply disturbed Zhang Jian, and he wrote to them immediately. The letter went “Do you resign one after another because you think your knowledge is limited for teaching, or because teaching is too hard? The improvement of learning lies with combination of theory and practice. Learning and teaching at the same time is the right way to make up for the shortage. So limited knowledge should not be the reason for your resignation. If you feel that teaching is too hard, I would like to show you my reflection.” Zhang Jian said, “I work hard like a beast of burden all the year round. I never say that I have worked hard even though I am busy all day long. Now it is the time of national crisis, only education can save the country and the people. I hope you able scholars will urge each other forward and help me to work hard for the development of education in Nantong.” Impressed by Zhang Jian's spirit, the three teachers continued to serve in the education field in Nantong and later made due contributions.

竞 会 五 洲 文 明

Competing and Cooperating with the Outside World

不明世界大势，不能解决一国问题

1909年9月1日，江苏省咨议局在南京召开成立大会，120位当选议员公推张謇担任了议长。当选议长张謇按例致辞，他的几句开场白让在场的议员有顿开茅塞之感，议员黄炎培在多年后这样回忆：“议长开幕词劈头几句：‘不明世界大势，不能解决一国问题。’议员多来自田间，听这几句，胸襟顿觉廓大。”

张謇在江苏省咨议局大会上讲话表达的是他一贯的主张，那就是“一个人办一个县的事情，就要有一个省的眼光，办一个省的事情就要有全国的眼光，办一个国家的事情要有世界的眼光。” 作为中国早期现代化的先驱者，张謇始终关注着世界经济社会发展的趋势，从世界大势中寻找贫弱的中国、偏狭的南通可能的发展机遇，发现可以借鉴的经验。

Running a Country Needs World Vision

On September 1, 1909, Jiangsu Provincial Advisory Bureau held its inaugural meeting in Nanjing, and 120 councilors elected Zhang Jian as the speaker. Speaker-elect Zhang Jian delivered his speech, and his opening words gave the councilors present a sense of enlightenment. Councilor Huang Yanpei recalled many years later, "Most of the members came from the fields, so when they heard these words, they felt that their minds were broadened."

Zhang Jian's speech at the general meeting of the Advisory Council of Jiangsu Province expressed his consistent assertion that "one should have a provincial vision to run a county, a national vision to run a province, and a world vision to run a country." As a pioneer of early modernization in China, Zhang Jian always paid attention to the trend of world economic and social development, searched for possible development opportunities for the poor and weak China and the remote Nantong city, and discovered the experiences that could be learned.

培育通商

张謇说："世界经济之潮流喷涌而至，同则存，独则亡，通则胜，塞则败。昔之为商，用吾习惯，可以闭门而自活。今门不可闭也，闭门则不可以自活。"张謇除了通过兴办工贸金融企业及商会、举行劝业展会活动培育人们的经商能力意识外，还创办商业学校和各种专修班，"养成吾通州开门商战人才"。

1911年，南通商业学校建成开学之时，张謇谆谆教导学生们说："今则万国交通，人以货来，占我市场，我退一步，则他人即进一步。在我则已退之步不能复，在人则务进不已，我将无地可容。天演公例，不进则退。我如何能不退？如何能进？此非有世界之观念与商战之知识不可。"张謇不断向学生们灌输着"列强竞争之时代"必须具备竞争意识，培养他们的商战精神，进而培养新一代具有现代商业精神的"通商"。

Training and Nurturing Nantong Merchants

Zhang Jian said, "The tide of the world economy surges up violently. Under this backdrop, cooperation leads to prosperity while isolation results in demise, and exchange leads to success while blockade results in failure. In the past, businessperson can survive behind closed door. But now we can't live by ourselves with doors closed." Zhang Jian not only cultivated people's awareness of business by setting up trade and financial enterprises, chambers of commerce and holding persuasive exhibitions, but also founded business schools and various special classes to "cultivate open-door business talents".

In 1911, when the Nantong Business School was opened, Zhang taught the students sagely: "Nowadays, foreign countries are exporting goods to China to occupy our market. If we retreat an inch, they will press on a mile. For us, the retreat cannot be restored; but for insatiable foreign countries, the occupation will never end until we have nowhere to retreat. It is the law of nature that those who don't advance will be left behind. How can we stop retreating? How can we advance? The answers for those questions lie in world vision and knowledge of business warfare." Zhang Jian constantly instilled in his students the need to have a sense of competition in the "era of competition among the powers", cultivated their spirit of business warfare, and thus nurtured a new generation of "Nantong merchants" with modern business spirit.

南通綉織局

纽约的南通绣织分局

第五大道（Fifth Avenue）是美国纽约市曼哈顿一条重要的南北向干道，位于曼哈顿岛的中心地带。第五大道在60街到34街之间的路段，被称为“梦之街”，这里聚集了许多著名的品牌商店，近百年来这里是全球租金最为昂贵的零售业场所之一。1920年，竟有一所来自中国南通的艺术品公司——南通绣织局分局在此开业了。

南通女红传习所自1914年成立以来，培养了一批刺绣人才，绣品亦多。为维持学校经费，解决女工生计，张謇创建了南通绣织局，从事绣品以及发网、花边等手工艺品经营，请沈寿兼任局长。为了“倡海外贸易，表示中国手工”，1920年，南通绣织局在纽约开办分局，在瑞士、意大利等地建立销售部，南通刺绣进入了国际市场。

Nantong Embroidery and Fabric Branch Office in New York

Fifth Avenue is a major north-south artery located in the heart of Manhattan, New York. The section of Fifth Avenue between 60th and 34th Streets, known as the “Street of Dreams”, is home to many famous branded stores and for nearly 100 years was one of the most expensive retail locations in the world. Nantong Embroidery and Fabric Shop were launched here in 1920.

After Nantong Women’s School for Needlework was established in 1914, a number of talents were cultivated and many embroideries were produced. In order to fund the school and provide jobs for female workers, Zhang Jian established Nantong Embroidery and Fabric Shop to engage in embroidery, hairnet, lace and other handicrafts. Shen Shou (famous embroidery craftsman) was entrusted by Zhang Jian to act as the director of the shop. To “advocate foreign trade and publicize Chinese handicraft”, Nantong Embroidery and Fabric Shop opened a branch in New York in 1920, and established sales departments in Switzerland and Italy. In doing so, Nantong embroidery entered the international market.

南通是獨一無二的在於它是全中國唯一在英文報紙上給自己做廣告的城市
THE WEEKLY REVIEW
37
INDUSTRIAL PROGRESS
IN CHINA
NANTUNGCHOW (THE MODEL CITY OF CHINA)

为南通做广告

张謇注重宣传城市形象。早在1910年，张謇就主持出版了英文版的《通州教育和实业图览》，通过100幅照片及说明文字对外介绍、宣传、推广南通。1915年，由翰墨林印书局出版了《地方自治十九年之成绩》，系统介绍了南通在实业、教育、慈善和地方自治方面的成就。1920年，又由上海商务印书馆出版了《南通工业、教育、慈善、风景，附旅行指南》，这一份图片丰富、中英文对照的风景图册，全面对外展示了南通——一个现代模范城市的形象。

1920年6月12日，英文周报《密勒氏评论报》上刊载了以《南通——中国模范城”（NANTUNGCHOW—The Model City of China）》为题的一整版城市广告。广告介绍了南通棉产、交通、学校、纺织、金融、外贸等11项发展成就。有美国传教士评述说："南通是独一无二的，在于它是全中国唯一在英文报纸上给自己做广告的城市。"

Advertising Nantong

Zhang Jian laid stress on promoting the image of the Nantong. As early as 1910, Zhang Jian hosted the publication of *Tongzhou Education and Industry Atlas* in English, which introduced, publicized and promoted Nantong to the public through 100 photos and explanatory texts. In 1915, *Nineteen Years of Local Self-governance* was published by Hanmolean Printing House, which systematically introduced the achievements of Nantong in industry, education, charity and local self-governance. In 1920, *Nantong Industry, Education, Charity and Scenery with Travel Guide* was published by Shanghai Commercial Press. This picture-rich landscape atlas in both Chinese and English comprehensively presented the image of Nantong, a modern model city, to the public.

On June 12, 1920, a full-page advertisement for Nantong with the title "NANTUNGCHOW – the Model City of China" was published in English weekly newspaper, *The Miller's Review*. The advertisement introduced 11 achievements of Nantong, including cotton production, transportation, schools, textiles, finance, and foreign trade. A missionary of the American Church of Christ commented, "Nantong is unique in that it is the only city in China that advertises itself in an English-language newspaper."

杜威评价南通教育

1920年6月5日至9日，美国著名教育家、哲学家杜威博士受南通县中等以上学校联合会邀请，到南通考察、讲学，成为近代南通中西文化交流史的重要一页。杜威在南通发表了三场演讲。6月6日上午，杜威在更俗剧场发表了第一场演讲。张謇在演讲之前致介绍辞，向聆听者表达了邀请杜威来南通的目的："博士于世界思潮，极力浚发，又能明白中国之政治关系及教育情状，甚为难得。南通僻处偏隅，不可不使教员学生亲博士之风采，聆博士之言论，以定适当之趋向。"南通的师范教育给杜威留下深刻印象，他在参观后的演讲中说："今兹一度游，觉此邦文物，吾后来殆眷恋不忘；而最足印吾心目中者，厥惟师范教育。"他对南通兴盛的教育事业寄予厚望："南通者，教育之源泉，吾尤望其成为世界教育之中心也。"

Dewey's Evaluation of Nantong Education

From June 5 to 9, 1920, Dr. Dewey, a famous American educator and philosopher, was invited by the Secondary and Higher Schools Association of Nantong County to visit and lecture in Nantong, which marked an important chapter in modern Nantong's cultural exchange with the West. In the morning of June 6, Dewey delivered his first lecture at the Gengsu Theatre. Before his speech, Zhang Jian made an introductory speech and expressed the purpose of inviting Dewey to Nantong, "It is very rare that Dr. Dewey is in the forefront of social change and is also able to understand the political relations and educational situation in China. As Nantong is located in a relatively remote place, our teachers and students must listen carefully to his remarks to take a pulse of today's world." Dewey was so impressed by the training of teachers in Nantong that he said in his speech after the visit, "I feel that I will never forget my visit to Nantong, and what impresses me most during the visit is the training of teachers." He had high hopes for the flourishing education in Nantong, "Nantong is the well-spring of education, and I especially hope that it will become the center of education in the world."

獨南通城市之經營張謇不倦其力宛然有爲江北一帶之首都之現象……

治世“良药”

1922年南通实业出现债务危机，张謇考虑向日本财团借款。1923年，受日本涩泽财团委托，驹井德三来南通进行了数月的调查，调查结果写成了《张謇关系事业调查报告书》。报告书对南通和张謇推崇备至：“惟公（张謇）独居南通，拥江北之区域，所怀之理想，数十年始终一贯，表面以分头于实业交通水利之建设，里面则醉心于教育及慈善事业之学理，乃唯一主新中国之创造者，诚可谓治现今中国社会之良药，而非过言者也。”驹井德三还这样评价南通：“独南通城市之经营，张謇不倦其力，宛然有为江北一带之首都之现象。”他认为南通建设的经验是“治现今中国社会之良药”。

Prescription for Governing the Country

In 1922, Nantong industry was in debt crisis, and Zhang Jian considered borrowing money from Japanese consortium. In 1923, entrusted by Japanese Shibusawa consortium, Takuzan Komai came to Nantong to conduct investigation for several months, and on this basis completed the *Report on the Investigation of Zhang Jian-related Undertakings*. The report praised Nantong and Zhang Jian, “Zhang Jian, living in Nantong, had great influence on the north of the Yangtze River. For decades, he has been committed to industry, transportation and water conservancy on the one hand, and education, philanthropy on the other hand. He is the one that champions the creation of the new China, offering prescription for governing the country.” Takuzo Komai commented that the city Nantong, through the relentless efforts of Zhangjian, showed the momentum to become the actual capital in the north of Yangtze River. Takuzo Komai considered the experience of Nantong “a good medicine for the present Chinese society”.

A Chinese View of Am
THE CHINA WEEKLY REVIEW
The China Weekly
REVIEW
報論評氏勒密

中国模范城

在张謇的领导下，从1895年起，经过30年的苦心经营，南通早期现代化建设已经达到一定水准，实业、教育、城市建设、地方自治、慈善公益等各种事业蓬勃兴起，南通已经从一个封闭落后的封建县邑逐步发展为闻名全国的近代化城市，被誉为“中国最进步的城市”。

“中国人间天堂”“中国模范城”“中国最出色城市”等对南通的赞誉，频繁出现在20世纪20年代的《字林西报》《大陆报》《密勒氏评论报》等著名的外文报纸上，其中以曾多次报道南通的《密勒氏评论报》最具代表性。1923年3月17日的《密勒氏评论报》上出现了以《中国实业之进步观——中国模范城南通州》为题的整版报道。各类媒体纷纷报道南通的建设成就，扩大了南通的影响力。

China's Model City

Through 30 years of painstaking efforts from 1895 to 1926 (the year when Zhang Jian passed way), Nantong had made great progress in modernization, and various undertakings such as industry, education, urban construction, local self-governance and charity flourished. Nantong had gradually developed from a closed and backward feudal county into a modernized city famous throughout China. It was known as "the most progressive city in China".

"China's Heaven on Earth," "China's Model City," "China's Most Outstanding City," and other acclaim frequently hit the English-language newspapers of the 1920s, such as *North China Daily News, China Press* and *The Millard's Review*. Among the newspapers that reported on Nantong, *The Millard's Review* was the most representative. A full-page report titled "The Industrial Progress made in China — China's Model City, Nantungchow" appeared in the March 17, 1923 issue of *The Millard's Review*. Various media reports on Nantong's achievements helped to widen its influence.

民族企业家的楷模
体育发展
家纺
铁军
科技
城市规划
南通教育

民族企业家的楷模

张謇曾说："天之生人也，与草木无异，若遗留一二有用事业，与草木同生，即不与草木同腐。故踊跃从公者，做一分便是一分，做一寸便是一寸。鄙人办事亦本此意。"张謇正是以这样的人生情怀和实干精神，以强毅之力行其志，给南通留下了一个规模庞大的民族资本集团、一个相对完整的教育体系、一套完善的城市设施、一系列公益慈善事业，开启了南通早期近代化进程。纵观张謇一生及其对民族、对国家所做的贡献，在张謇身上彰显出爱国、创新、诚信、社会责任、国际视野等五个方面的精神。2020年7月21日，习近平总书记在企业家座谈会上赞扬张謇是"爱国企业家的典范"。11月12 日，习总书记在南通博物苑调研视察时说："张謇是中国民营企业家的先贤和楷模。"习近平总书记对张謇的评价，是对张謇一生事业的高度概括。

A Paragon of Patriotism, A Model of Entrepreneurship

Zhang Jian once said, "The people on earth are no different from grass and trees. But if they can leave behind some useful causes, they will not rot with grass and trees. Therefore, those who are eager to serve the public should do your utmost. This is also my rule of life." With such life philosophy and practical spirit, Zhang Jian carried out his will with great perseverance. His legacy includes a large-scale enterprise group, a relatively complete education system, a set of perfect urban facilities and a series of public welfare and charitable undertakings, which initiated early modernization of Nantong. Throughout his life, he made great contribution to the nation and the country, and embadied such qualities as patriotism, innovation, integrity, social responsibility and embodied international vision. On July 21, 2020, President Xi Jinping acclaimed him as "Paragon of Patriotic Entrepreneur" on the Forum of Entrepreneurs. On November 12, President Xi Jinping said, "Zhang Jian is the sage and model for Chinese private entrepreneurs" during his inspection in Nantong Museum. President Xi's comment on Zhang Jian is a high praise of his lifetime undertakings.

百年梦圆

百年前的南通，经过张謇等人的努力，从一个落后的封建县邑发展成为“模范县”。百年后的南通，经济繁荣、科教发达、人文荟萃，成为闻名遐迩的纺织之乡、建筑之乡、教育之乡、体育之乡、长寿之乡、文博之乡、平安之乡、新侨之乡。先后诞生了两院院士47位，世界体育冠军21位。2020年，南通地区生产总值突破1万亿元。习近平总书记视察南通时说，大家生活在这样的城市里很幸福。

潮平两岸阔，风正一帆悬。勤劳勇敢智慧的江海儿女，在中国共产党领导下，正以新的奋斗姿态，将张謇先生的家乡建设得更加美好，为实现中华民族伟大复兴的中国梦贡献南通力量。

Fulfilling Life-time Dream

A hundred years ago, Nantong developed from a backward feudal county into a “model county” through the efforts of Zhang Jian and others. A hundred years later, Nantong has become a world-famous city for its construction capacity, primary education, cultural heritage as well as homegrown sports champions and long-lived citizens. Boasting of economic prosperity, scientific and educational development and rich cultural heritage, it is home to 47 academicians and 21 world sports champions. In 2020, the GDP of Nantong exceeded 1 trillion yuan. When inspecting Nantong, General Secretary Xi Jinping said that everyone was happy to live in such a city.

Under the leadership of the Chinese Communist Party, the hard-working, brave and intelligent people of Nantong are gaining new momentum to build Zhang Jian’s hometown into a better place, and make their contribution to realize the Chinese dream of the great rejuvenation of the Chinese nation.

后记

张謇在中国近代史上具有不凡的影响力，他是国内众多学者争相研究、记述的重要对象，相关论文书籍可谓卷帙浩繁、汗牛充栋，当中更有张謇先生的后人亲自编纂的精美画册和专业著作。因此，以小篇幅的图文讲述张謇故事是一件很困难的事。幸而，我们得到了张謇曾孙张慎欣先生的帮助，他欣然答应担任顾问，给予大力支持和精心指导，促成了本书能在较短的时间内得以顺利出版。

本书概述了张謇先生人生传略，重点展示张謇在国家内忧外患之时，穷且益坚、不坠青云之志，依靠信念和奋斗干成了诸多颇具开创性且有益于社会之事。在这些故事中，我们真切地感受到了奋斗、担当、创新等关键词的力量，以及浓浓的人文情怀。这些也是中华传统文化的优秀因子，是中国故事之中的精神力量。正因如此，我们以中英文对照的形式呈现，并将在后期加大国际传播，让海内外更多朋友来一起分享。

本书的编创工作得到了社会各界专家朋友的指点和帮助，在此一并表示感谢。

编者

2021年7月

Postscript

With powerful influence in modern history of China, Zhang Jian is a focus of research among many domestic scholars. There have been a huge number of books and papers about him, and the descendants of Zhang Jian have also compiled albums and monographs about him. Therefore, it is very difficult to tell the story of Zhang Jian using comics with limited length of article. Fortunately, we got great support and guidance from Mr. Zhang Shenxin, Zhang Jian's great-grandson, who gladly acted as a consultant for this book and contributed a lot to the editing and publication of this book.

This comic book outlines the life of Zhang Jian, highlighting his tenacity in saving the nation in face of domestic disturbance and foreign aggression. Throughout his life, Zhang made a lot of pioneering efforts that benefited the society and the people. In his stories, the key words of hard work, responsibility, and innovation, as well as humanistic care, stand out. These are also the elements of Chinese traditional culture and the spiritual power of China. We present this book in both Chinese and English, sharing the story of Zhang Jian with readers both in and out of China.

We would like to express our gratitude to all the experts and friends who have offered advice and help to the editing of this book.

Editors

July 2021

图书在版编目 (CIP) 数据
漫话张謇: 汉英对照/中共南通市委网信办编. —
北京: 外文出版社, 2021.8
ISBN 978-7-119-12812-2
Ⅰ. ①漫… Ⅱ. ①中… Ⅲ. ①张謇（1853-1926）－生平事迹－通俗读物－汉、英 Ⅳ. ①K825.38-49
中国版本图书馆CIP数据核字(2021)第185116号

编 委 会: 俞 雷 赵明远 成继唐 马佩军 张光明 陈全红 李 勇
顾　　问: 张慎欣
主　　编: 俞 雷
副 主 编: 赵明远
撰　　稿: 赵明远 吴昊翔
漫　　画: 蔡 欣
英文翻译: 吴小佩
英文审定: 魏园林 侯福莉
责任编辑: 蔡莉莉
书籍设计: 潘振宇 774038217@qq.com
印刷监制: 章云天
编　　务: 吕 建 宋代志 沈洪斌 张庆辉 吴 飞 许晓燕 邹国童 李春华 施帅杰 吴燕南 吴韵洁 佘 俣 沈怡柔 张 伟 郑 珉

漫话张謇　中共南通市委网信办 编

出 版 人: 胡开敏
出版发行: 外文出版社有限责任公司
地　　址: 北京市西城区百万庄大街24号
邮政编码: 100037
网　　址: http://www.flp.com.cn
电子邮箱: flp@cipg.org.cn
电　　话: 008610-68320579（总编室）
008610-68996167（编辑部）
008610-68995852（发行部）
008610-68327750（版权部）
印　　刷: 鸿博昊天科技有限公司
经　　销: 新华书店/外文书店
开　　本: 787×1092mm 1/16
印　　张: 10.5
版　　次: 2021年10月第1版第1次印刷
书　　号: ISBN 978-7-119-12812-2
定　　价: 128.00元